# MYTHS THAT MIRE THE MINISTRY

Rev. & Mrs. Pleasant

Joy

September 4, 1985

Rev.
Harold G. Carter

Peace!

# MYTHS THAT MIRE THE MINISTRY

## HAROLD A. CARTER

Judson Press ® Valley Forge

**MYTHS THAT MIRE THE MINISTRY**

Copyright © 1980
Judson Press, Valley Forge, PA 19481

Unless otherwise indicated, Bible quotations in this volume are from *The Holy Bible*, King James Version.

**Library of Congress Cataloging in Publication Data**

Carter, Harold A.
    Myths that mire the ministry.

    Includes bibliographical references.
    1.  Clergy—Office.    2.   Pastoral theology.
I.  Title.
BV660.2.C35        253'.2        79-9338
ISBN 0-8170-0845-4

The name JUDSON PRESS is registered as a trademark in the U.S. Patent Office.
Printed in the U.S.A. ✣

*To loving members, ministers, "Sons of the Prophet" of New Shiloh Baptist Church, "A Church Determined to Live with Christ."*

# Contents

# Preface

The Christian ministry evokes the deepest emotion of my life. The genesis of this emotion I owe to the home in which I grew up in Selma, Alabama. I was the third of five children in the home of Rev. and Mrs. Nathan Mitchell Carter. My father, a Baptist pastor, preacher, and professor, spent the bulk of his time as an instructor in the classroom of Selma University, a Baptist school located in Selma. My earliest educational training occurred at this school, where adults and youth often sat side by side in classrooms.

This school, founded in 1878 by Baptists of Alabama, reached out to train all persons, especially those in the Christian ministry. Many ministers came to the school with no formal educational training whatsoever. Many of them became my friends in elementary, junior, and high school levels. I learned a great deal about ministerial life, its problems, joys, expectations, and fulfillments in countless conversations and buzz sessions. What minister was having problems in the church and why was always a provoker of discussions. How various members sought to control the church and even order the pastor around were dramatic sources of conversation and human interest.

My sponge-like mind soaked up many interesting words conveyed by my older friends. I heard them talking about the problems and pitfalls of alcohol, seductive women, prestige fights, and thievery of church funds. I listened with interest to the spontaneous sermons that often burst forth under shade trees in the springtime. It appeared to me then that some ministers wanted their friends to think of them as burning human vessels, alive with the message of God. Others seemed to want their friends to see them as czars, reigning potentates of their churches. There was still another group who seemed to be quiet, studious, and persons of few words. All of them were my friends and were making lasting impressions upon me.

My home was the place where ministerial personalities and problems were discussed and placed in some meaningful perspective. My father, a teacher of Bible and theology, possessed a love for ministers that colored all of his comments and critical judgments of the clergy. Whatever weaknesses the ministry had, Daddy always found some good virtue in its life. He always saw the other side of the minister's problems. My brother, my three sisters, and I often took Daddy to task for what we saw as the Christian ministry's serious weaknesses and unfulfilled commitments to the people. Still the balanced positions to ministerial problems articulated by my father caused me to reflect soberly upon and reach conclusions about the very calling I would one day enter and expound.

We debated the question of whether the minister needed formal education to be successful. We discussed the churches that had been led by a trained ministry but had shifted to an untrained ministry during times of transitions. Was it the people who cared less for education and more for ministerial style? We discussed the spiritually gifted ministers who, with apparent ease, could move congregations with powerful oratory. Did this gift render unnecessary their need for rigorous theological accomplishments? Naturally we compared their gifts with persons who applied themselves scholastically but had not the same powers of oral communication and preaching persuasion. How do you get one full of the spirit to know he or she needs the disciplines of the letter, meaning a thorough theological education?

Years later, after I had accepted the call into the Christian ministry, I had these past conversations to ponder and sift through. In seminary I expected to study Bible, church history, ethics, and theology. All of these courses were extremely helpful and certainly enlarged my mind. However, many of the concerns I heard my older friends talking about at Selma University never surfaced in the seminary classroom. I never heard the instructor in Christian ethics lecture on the basic morality that ought to be part and parcel of the Christian ministry. Pastoral counseling classes often turned attention to others and overlooked the minister's home, the place where his or her final effectiveness rises or falls. Theology classes often shifted to systematic studies of God and his attributes and overlooked the necessity of the minister's devotional life as a prime requisite for a true and realistic knowledge of God. In a word, many of the weightier ministerial concerns lay dormant throughout my seminary ministerial training.

Today, nineteen years after receiving a Bachelor of Divinity degree from Crozer Theological Seminary, Chester, Pennsylvania, and doctoral degrees from Colgate Rochester Seminary, Rochester, New York, and St. Mary's Ecumenical Seminary, Baltimore, Maryland, and having served two pastorates, one in Lynchburg, Virginia, and the other in Baltimore, Maryland, I have decided to write this book. I want to lift up concerns I believe are pitfalls for effective Christian ministry. I believe the fellowship of Christian ministry can be strengthened by an intellectual dialogue of problems peculiar to this work.

Three phases of my ministry have added to the strength of this work. A brief period of ministry among migrant farm workers in Genesee County, New York, eventuated in the building of a church and provided me initial experiences in working with people. Two urban ministries, Court Street Baptist Church, Lynchburg, Virginia, 1959–1964, and the New Shiloh Baptist Church, Baltimore, Maryland, where I now pastor, have placed me strategically in the heart of Christian ministry where a great deal of action has taken place and still does even to this day. In both pastorates, I have experienced local church, community wide, and national commitments in the faith. Young ministers have grown up out of both pastorates, with sixteen ministers growing out of the present pasture in Baltimore alone! Eight of them have now received churches and are involved in college, seminary, and post-seminary training. This kind of broad-based ministry has permitted me to travel widely, to address national gatherings of denominational bodies, and to gain insight from working with social and civic organizations.

I worked a full year as pastoral assistant to Dr. Martin Luther King, Jr. I value the marriage of proclamation to human reclamation I saw in his ministry. His sense of openness to work with all the people of God enlarged my own concern to do an effective ministry for all persons. This concern has led me to minister to Catholics, Jews, Blacks, and Whites. I therefore feel a certain burden to share the essence of ministerial judgments and experiences with others who follow in the procession of faith.

This work is not intended to be a final scholarly journal on the Christian ministry. In many ways it is based largely on the circumstantial and experiential development I have received. I believe it will meet a definite need of many Christian workers inside and outside of pulpit ministries. It will attempt to speak frankly to problems that otherwise might go unanswered. Each minister is called upon to serve this present age. If, in some way, this work helps them do that, this labor of love will certainly not have been in vain.

# Introduction

# 1

The myths that mire the ministry are dressed in angel garb. They are communicated in the oral traditions of one minister to another. They are expressed and often practiced in associational meetings, state and national conventions, where Christians gather to conduct religious business. The influence they have in shaping and molding the lives and thought patterns of the minister is awesome. Because they are silently associated with these gatherings, they seem to have official sanction. Until they are seriously identified and dealt with, a major hindrance to ministerial development will haunt those who fall prey to their sinister traps.

The use of the term "myth" will refer to an accepted belief where a degree of truth is interlocked with error. For example, it is reported by Paul that he had a thorn in the flesh. Mythological judgments of this thorn in the flesh have ranged from the idea that Paul was sexually deviant all the way to the idea that he had some paralysis of his body; these ideas are generally colored by the persons who seek to advance them. All too often the suppositions have become stronger than the basic truth, that Paul had a thorn in the flesh. All the myths of this study have some basis in truth but are colored by human error, growing out of human weaknesses and failure to commit one's life to the best we find in Christ.

The myths we will deal with include the notion that a call from God completes one's ministerial requirements. A second myth will deal with the problem of charisma and how spiritual images are often used to hide the lack of biblical substance and theological foundations. The concupiscence myth will not be overlooked. It deals with the ageless problem of free sex and lustful living. The church control myth will be discussed in an effort to show that the minister is a servant and not a god-like dictator of the powerful Word of God. Besides the church control myth, we will discuss the children's charmer myth; dealing with this myth is especially important today because we seem to be so obsessed with paying attention to youth that we have overlooked some fundamental needs and principles for this vulnerable age group. That the minister is no civic leader for various and sundry activities will be explored. The minister's relationship to life generally will be explored finally under the careless, carefree myth.

It will be demonstrated that all these myths are powerful and strangely interrelated. Part of their power comes from the espousal they receive from elderly ministers. "Don't worry about a lot of study and the delivery of scholarly sermons," many a minister has said to some younger person. "All the folks want to hear is something about Jesus. Remember how Paul flunked on Mars Hill. After Mars Hill he knew nothing but Jesus Christ and him crucified!" On the surface the minister has provided a powerful frame of reference for the young mind and stands as a model to be followed and emulated. Great truth appears to be a part of this utterance. The simplest mind knows Jesus is the central force of our faith. However, all the time the statement covers up the necessity for study and mental discipline—all necessary just to know Jesus! It also appeals to the latent appetite for laziness and results in the loss of pulpit excellence which ought to be the goal of every pastor.

There are three major sources of knowledge open to all ministers. They are information gained from others, inside and outside classrooms; experience gained from traffic in life; and revelation gained from Almighty God. No attempt will be made to play down any of these sources of knowledge, but rather it will be shown how all of them are vitally needed. Renewed attention has been given to the church in these latter years of the twentieth century. Scholars of all persuasions are taking a new look at the life of the historic Jesus. Persons who fill the pews of churches need more than an emotional charge once a week to live and grow upon. Clearly needed is a ministry that is aware of the pitfalls of the faith and is solidly anchored in the ministry of God's Word that is both rational and articulate.

The insights presented in this book will draw from personal experiences, widespread travel, shared experiences and dialogues with influential Christian leaders. The Bible will be a major source book. Some attention will also be given to authors whose studies amplify and clarify specific points. Some interviews with pastors and theologians will furnish additional helpful information.

Anyone entering the Christian ministry is faced with an almost unbearable burden. One has to face the concepts one has of this work, that may or may not run counter to the demands of Christ. This was a common problem for the apostles. Over and over again their idea of what Christian ministry should be had to be radically redirected by the leadership of Christ. One must also face the many images the world has about the ministry. Some of these images are openly hostile, embarrassing, and even confusing. Ministers have been called "jackleg preachers," "self-proclaimed leaders," and even "rip-off artists who stole in the name of the Lord." Finding the right anchor and relating oneself to the right image is a problem of no small concern.

Many young ministers, anxious for quick success, have consistently sought to imitate the ways of their pastors. Even this approach has problems. There is always the danger the young minister will not be able to differentiate strengths and weaknesses in the one being idolized. Furthermore, it takes time, study, and theological and biblical growth for the newly called minister to command the respect and following the pastor does. Neither does the congregation accept the words, actions, styles, and mannerisms of the young minister as being genuinely real in the same sense as the elder leader. The young minister needs to know the various images, beliefs, and expectations people have about the ministry. No harm will come from studying in depth the life and style of the one being idolized, providing one has the sense to go on and develop the depths and strengths of one's own personality and calling. Ministers do gain from one another, but they always develop their fuller selves only in their relationship with Jesus Christ.

Our task will demand a straightforward approach to the problems raised. Personal opinions will be presented where necessary so that the reader will not be left in doubt. Dealing with the myths already referred to will require a genuine effort to be truthful, speak frankly, and lay open issues that need discussion and Christian concern.

The impact of the Watergate revelations in the administration of Mr. Richard Nixon started what continues to be a far-reaching effort to make sure that the lives of political leaders are filled with moral integrity. Politicians make no pretense of being Christian ministers; still they know they cannot long serve the people through slander and distortion of the public trust. They have seen what hidden corruption can do when brought to light. A certain amount of fortitude and public pressure was needed to break the growing idea of political invincibility in our nation. The pressure came because wrong cannot forever enthrone itself. In our times, politicians have had to come to terms with their work, their mission, and the people to be served.

The Christian ministry should be no less responsible to the people of God. The fact that the minister is finally answerable only to God for one's actions demands a Christian maturity of the highest caliber. Ministerial practices made popular through long years of tradition and hardened custom do not necessarily sanctify their continued use.

Every minister needs to ask oneself: Where do I go after I am called to preach? How do I become a meaningful extension of the word of God? How do I relate in a positive way to God's revelation for my day and generation? Ministers of yesterdays may have been forced to serve without formal training. Schools and libraries were not always available. God, out of his amazing grace, had ways to circumvent their shortcomings and made many Christian warriors of bygone days mighty in the faith. Many of the elders were able to take the call to preach and move with blazing fire across the lives of the people of God. They served well their day and generation.

Every generation needs to build on the strengths of the preceding one. This is profoundly true of the Christian minister. We serve a God of progressive revelation. Our mission always moves from Egypt to Canaan, from Galilee to Jerusalem. Therefore, the ministry must wisely receive the spiritual legacies of yesterday. Yesterday's generations bequeathed to us a sense of the immediacy of God in the affairs of human life. The work ethic was equated to holy responsibility before God. The Bible was received as God's Holy Word, truly inspired and without error in its message of truth. The preaching of the Word was always the central force around which the people of God gathered. The minister of yesterday believed that, when he spoke, somehow the voice of God spoke through him. We need to receive and build upon all these positive virtues and more.

But we must not permit the glory of yesterday to cause us to neglect the struggles mandated upon us for today. Vast numbers of ministers today are led to believe that preaching is simply rapping with style and does not need too much substance. Some have not seen and appreciated that theological growth is a prime requisite for enlarging the people of God. Too often public images and ministerial styles take precedence over the eternal way of the cross! Preaching is reduced to "gift" and has not much to do with breaking the Bread of Life.

This work invites the reader to think through these problems. Christianity is serious business, requiring the utmost of personal attention and devotion. In the following pages, that kind of attention and devotion will be offered to the problems presented. Together we will gain strength, as we seek a fuller knowledge of our God.

# The Call Completed Myth

# 2

And he said unto me, Son of man, stand upon thy feet, and I will speak unto thee. And the spirit entered into me when he spake unto me, and set me upon my feet, that I heard him that spake unto me (Ezekiel 2:1-2).

Wherefore the rather, brethren, give diligence to make your calling and election sure: for if ye do these things, ye shall never fall (2 Peter 1:10).

There is no testimony in the minister's arsenal greater than the affirmation that "God has called me to preach his Word." Inherent in this statement is the proclamation that God has honored my lowly estate and communed with me face to face. Suddenly I have been called to be a living mouthpiece for God. I have been singled out like Abraham, from family, kindred, and countrymen about me, to be an ambassador of God's Word. I have been lifted to the company of Old Testament seers and prophets who declared to Israel and the world, "Thus saith the Lord." Like the fisherman Peter and the tax collector Matthew, I have left one vocation to follow a higher calling, after seeing and hearing the Savior from Galilee.

Almost instantaneously, I am not the person I was yesterday. Whatever failings may have haunted my life, they are now swept away by a mighty act of God. All who knew me must now reappraise their evaluations of my life. I am a living example of Amos, a herder of sycamore trees who left the farms of South Israel to be a prophet of God in Northern Israel. Henceforth my life will never be the same.

Historically, there has always existed the possibility for deception in the proclaimed call to divine ministry. The Old Testament was constantly plagued with prophets hired by the state and not inspired by God. These prophets, a counterfeit of true prophecy, were used by the king to support unpopular decisions and ratify military campaigns. A classic story of true and false prophecies occurred in the encounter of Ahab, king of Israel, and Jehoshaphat, king of Judah. "And Ahab king of Israel said unto Jehoshaphat king of Judah, Wilt thou go with me to Ramoth-gilead?" (2 Chronicles 18:3). Ahab, at that time more powerful than his brother in the South, expected and received a positive answer. Only one question remained. Would Yahweh bless this battle? "Therefore the king of Israel gathered together of prophets four hundred men, and said unto them, Shall we go to Ramoth-gilead to battle, or shall I forbear? And they said, Go up; for God will deliver it into the king's hand" (2 Chronicles 18:5). Further inquiry by the king brought forth a man of God not tied to the court, by the name of Micaiah. The king's own words revealed the tension between true prophets of God and those appointed by the kingdom.

> And the king of Israel said unto Jehoshaphat, There is yet one man, by whom we may inquire of the LORD: but I hate him; for he never prophesied good unto me, but always evil: the same is Micaiah the son of Imla. . . . And the messenger that went to call Micaiah spake to him, saying, Behold, the words of the prophets declare good to the king with one assent; let thy word therefore, I pray thee, be like theirs, and speak thou good (2 Chronicles 18:7, 12).

Micaiah, led by a higher authority, spoke the truth of God and declared the impending judgment that was going to fall upon the armies of Israel. He was convinced that his allegiance was not to self, nor to the king's court, nor to the false prophets about him, but totally to God. This man of God stood against solid opposition that even threatened the security and well-being of his own life.

This Old Testament story depicts the potentially serious problem that often arises when one proclaims, "God has called me to preach." Since God is not usually questioned about such proclamation, the burden of evidence rests with the minister. This means the authenticity of one's calling is based largely upon one's sincerity. The world has never devised a workable guideline to separate a genuine call from God from a call initiated by the cunning craftiness of humankind. Ultimately we rest upon the utterance of Jesus who stated, "By their fruits ye shall know them" (Matthew 7:20). To delve further into this question, let us explore some thoughts about the preacher often held in the minds of the people.

## Some Ideas About the Call Among the People

The lawyer is expected to choose to practice law out of a love for social justice, the concern of legal science, and the honest desire to serve in the human arena. The doctor is expected to choose medicine to serve people and to fulfill the needs of one's person. Travelers on modern-day jets board the big ships with an almost childlike faith in the pilot's abilities to handle the craft and land it safely at the desired destination. People generally believe all of these vocations demand highly motivated and qualified persons, willing to do serious study and to excel in their fields. When we add the Christian ministry to this list of vocations, something happens in the thinking of the masses. There is the widespread and deeply ingrained belief that almost anyone can take up this work. There are no rigid standards that bar one from becoming at once a minister of this faith. No long-range goals are required of the minister to attain public acclaim or success. Whatever shortcuts may be used to reach the top are often part of the rush for public acceptance. Interestingly enough, people expect confidential and reliable services from their lawyers, doctors, and airline pilots, but are exceedingly tolerant of those whom they trust to pilot their souls through the maze of life.

"This person looks like a preacher!" The public is apt to use these words to describe one whose physical style and features resemble some older minister. The older model, male or female, may have been a powerful person in the community and the church. Children growing up would certainly have felt the magnetizing pull of this sage, highly venerated by the people. Under this influence, it would be natural for the sensitive child to follow the behavior patterns of this powerful, godly person. Members of the local church congregation, anxious to insure the survival, even a kind of reincarnation of the beloved pastor, will say to the young person who seems to fit the

pastor's mold, "Child, you are sure to be a preacher." Sometimes
people will refer to that special style and behavior as "God's peculiar
mark" that sets one apart for the ministry. All this means that the one
entering the Christian ministry must raise the questions: "Am I
entering the ministry because of the voices of the people all around
me? Can I conclude that the voices of the people comprise the
unmistakable voice of God?"

Styles and images are not marks alien to the biblical record. Moses
was described as a proper son worthy of protection for the Lord's
work (Exodus 2:2). Esther, a woman of God, stood far above her
compatriots in the land of Babylon and eventually saw the king
(Esther 2:7-8). The Old Testament prophets were generally known for
their rustic look, long hair, and rugged outdoor appearances. John
the Baptist reminded the people of prophetic utterances and styles.
"John had his raiment of camel's hair, and a leathern girdle about his
loins; and his meat was locusts and wild honey" (Matthew 3:4).

Looking like a preacher is not a liability to the one called by God.
The problem lies in the attempt to find meaning and power in one's
looks, overlooking the weightier matters of faith. Samson, the strong
man of Old Testament life, trusted the muscular powers of his limbs
and overlooked the weightier matters of faith, to his own defeat.
Looks and images properly understood and used can always be a
blessing. They provide needed avenues for public acceptance and
positive work. They help to eliminate the necessity for one to prove
oneself and the Christ one represents. But if one's call to serve people
is no deeper than the collective voices of the people, one's ministry
will surely be buffeted by the fickle temperaments of the people one
serves.

There is always a tendency for ministers who have done the least
preparation for their divine calling to shout the loudest, "The Lord
has called me to this work!" This is a proclamation of authority
among the people and within ministerial ranks. This statement has
always been with us and will certainly not go away now. The one who
utters it must remember that each generation is finally grading each
minister in the light of works that matter and basically lift humanity.
History, in spite of the easy acceptance of those who enter ministerial
ranks, has a way of judging the good from the bad, the Micaiahs from
the sham court prophets.

Nomadic unlettered preachers of yesterday had history on their side when they cried out, "The Lord has called me to preach!" We today must seek to understand the context under which many of them spoke. Some were slaves, released from physical bondage, and deprived of educational opportunities. Some were poor Southerners, separated likewise from schools and theological opportunities. Out of this limited academic environment a positive affirmation of the anointment of God upon the life of his servant was received and affirmed. The illumination of God's will inherent in the call produced servants of amazing mental and biblical powers. No doors to formal education were conveniently available. There was no time to formulate systematic theologies or to structure coherent moral philosophies. People groped in darkness and needed to hear about Jesus. Churches needed to be founded. Souls in numerous valleys, plantations, small towns, and village hamlets had to be saved. There was a kind of race with time to get the ever-living story told before it was too late. Thus many of yesterday's itinerant preachers and pastors labored with the philosophy caught up in the slave song, "Didn't my Lord deliver Daniel; why not every man?" Clearly yesterday's call to minister carried with it a far different level of content and commitment than the call to minister today. In a word, the need for divine liberation and salvation of all persons remains the same, but the leadership for liberation and salvation lays upon God's servants today decisive demands which are far different from the demands of yesterday.

People today have a basic right to expect more of God's minister than uttered words devoid of thorough preparation. They have a right to expect God's minister to be fully equipped to serve not only the needs of the doctor, lawyer, and pilot, but also of everyone. If the vision of the minister is blurred, the people of God will suffer. "Where there is no vision, the people perish" (Proverbs 29:18). In dealing with the holy, calling persons to justice, righteousness, truth, and love, many will seek the easiest way out. Many persons will seek, like Old Testament kings, prophets of ease who will comfort them in their ungodly ways. Therefore Christian ministers must see their role as a kind of universal service, where, through preparation and dedication to Christ, they can serve all the people of God, people from every walk of life.

## The Problem of Instant Revelation

Revelation is the self-disclosure of God to his people. It is God's way of breaking through to humanity through whatever medium God chooses to use. Revelation has traditionally been seen as an intimate aspect of one's call to the gospel ministry. Chief among those mediums of revelation have been the voice of God in nature, the lessons of history, the personal experiences of God's holy word, the preaching of the gospel, and the person of the Lord Jesus Christ.

As we read the accounts of the biblical stars, called by God to the ministry, we tend to lift up the side of instant revelation while overlooking the long hours and years of hard preparation. The biblical account always kept revelation and preparation side by side. Abraham, the father of the faithful, was called by God and received in that call a powerful revelation. That revelation commanded him to do something. He had to leave country, kindred, and family, and go seeking a land, learning about God, literally discovering the nature of God each step of the way. This man of God was theologically trained by the matchless Teacher of the ages, as he saw salvation's plan unfold for his generation and future generations, step by step. Moses had received the finest education Egypt had to offer, before fleeing to the land of Midian: "To assure her dominance, she trained enterprising young courtiers in the intricacies of her own hieroglyphic and hieratic scripts as well as in the Assyro-Babylonian, Hittite, and Ugaritic cuneiform of the neighboring nations."[1] It is doubtful Moses would have had the place of power he commanded in Egypt without a thorough education in keeping with one who served in Pharaoh's court. His later quiet and meditative education in the household of Jethro, his priestly father-in-law, provided Moses with long years of reflective thought as he pondered the possibilities for the liberation of his people in Egypt.

In the New Testament, Mark left us these words: "And he goeth up into a mountain, and calleth unto him whom he would: and they came unto him. And he ordained twelve, that they should be with him, and that he might send them forth to preach" (Mark 3:13). Christ wanted these men to receive more than instant revelation. Their entire surroundings were a positive picture of disciples learning from the Master. They climbed a mountain to hear the Lord, suggestive of a new foundation. They spent meaningful hours on that mountain, learning the beatitudes, the ways and methods of missions, and discovering the unfolding powers of the Holy Spirit to reclaim the lives of humanity. They were instructed in order to go forth and empower others to minister with gospel tools.

The problem of instant revelation in our times may be due to the pressure to make the Christian faith compatible with other offerings of modern life. If food can be ordered and served without delay, why not religion? If modern drugs are expected to provide instant cures to human maladies, why not religion? After all, communication is practically instantaneous, and transportation is space age fast! Should ministers really have to prod along, year after year, simply preparing to tell others that Jesus is the Son of God?

The divine call to follow the way of God is the oldest of all words spoken to humanity. By its very nature, religious faith is conservative. It is a repository of the past, a recounting of the great acts of God, and humankind's response to those acts. It demands a basic knowledge of important events God has unfolded in order to interpret properly the acts of God in the now. Any instant revelation that circumvents the past experiences of the patriarchs, matriarchs, and saints who walked with God is suspect from the beginning. Humanity likes to deal in segments of time and quite often responds only with a knowledge of time as one sees it, while God deals in matters of eternity. There is no biblical precedent for instant revelation that does not take full account of one's past, present, and future. It is in this context that one struggles to make one's calling and election sure.

God does call his servants in time, and they are expected to serve their age and generation. The revelation is only a starting point. It may be compared to a pilot revving the engines of his plane before taking off for distant lands. The engine is revved to make sure all systems are going. So the minister must gladly receive the revelation, but must go on and properly prepare and set in order the systems of faith. A long pilgrimage of human deliverance awaits the servant of God.

## The Problem of Instant Ministerial Maturity

When instant revelation is received as an end in itself, any need for further educational and spiritual growth is ruled out. The natural growing and developing process of meaningful encounters with God through the lives of historical characters as well as the prophetic judgment of events affecting one's own time are usually lost. The one ingredient needed most to do the work of Christ, Christian maturity, is sacrificed for short-lived gains.

> There are many men who think in meetings that they are called to be teachers, and are divinely inspired, simply because they are conscious of a rush of feeling, of an intense action of their own mind. . . . But when a man, rattlebrained, without any experience in life, with nothing in him but conceit, and enough of that to make up for all other lackings, rises, and insists that he is called of the Spirit of God to teach, we all listen and say, "*What* has the Spirit of God called you to teach? Nonsense? Silliness?" Does God take the trouble to ordain a fool to come forward and tell us things that every infant in the nursery knows?[2]

Maturity in the gospel ministry demands more than a kind of spiritual halo around one's countenance. Looking like a holy person and talking and walking like a holy person are essentially functions of the body. These things do not shield the emptiness of one's mind and the shallowness of one's faith from the people.

The great prophets of Israel had young men around them who aspired for that noble work. Elisha was a great example. The young men around him built a seminary in the wilderness, where they could learn the lessons from their master. Prophetic succession was due a great deal to the transmission of knowledge from one master to another. The same kind of spiritual succession was seen in the ministry of Paul in the New Testament. To his son in the ministry Paul wrote, ". . . stir up the gift of God, which is in thee by the putting on of my hands" (2 Timothy 1:6). Paul wanted Timothy to grow, to become spiritually broad-minded, and to possess an expanding vision of the great things he could do in the service of Jesus Christ. Paul left Timothy with one of the basic rules for Christian maturity: "Study to shew thyself approved unto God, a workman that needeth not to be ashamed, rightly dividing the word of truth" (2 Timothy 2:15).

It is also interesting to observe some of the reasons Paul advanced in telling Timothy to be strong. Paul told him that in addition to the laying on of his hands, he had gifts that were biologically a part of his family tree (2 Timothy 1:5). He had the influence of a master teacher, preacher, and theologian in Paul himself (2 Timothy 1:6). He had his own unique call to preach the gospel of salvation through Jesus Christ the Lord (2 Timothy 4:1-2).

Paul did not advise Timothy to be like himself in every detail, but rather to abide in the faith Paul had lifted up. The richness of Timothy's own place in the faith had to be developed. Every fruit should ripen after its own kind. Some fruit may ripen sooner than others, but that is the nature of the tree. The Christian ministry, while universal in scope, still has a particular place for every person. No two persons in the Christian ministry need be exactly alike. The exciting, adventuresome, fulfilling romance of faith is a fact because God calls each of us to develop our fullest selves, in the molding power of his redeeming grace.

Some basic questions will help the minister keep his or her growth in focus: Who called me to this gospel ministry? Was I attracted to this work because of the advice of my pastor or some other person? Would I be happier in some other field of endeavor? Am I a minister because failure has overtaken me in some other vocation and instant success is now mine to claim? Am I now in this work till death do me part? "A few years ago there was a slogan among Southern Baptists expressed by this line: 'Calling Out the Called.' . . . There was danger of filling the ministry with men who were following the call of men rather than the call of the Lord."[3]

There is no substitute for the authentic call of Christ to the redemptive work of the minister. The local pastor, Christian worker, and people generally are often used by God to awaken faith in the ministers to the call God has for them to do. God has given us the fellowship of the church, the Body of Christ, to assist our spiritual growth. When the face of Christ is lost and his voice no longer heard, all other substitutes for the call to preach will bog down in religious quicksand. A deep and undying urgency of sincerity to do the will of God has proven to be the best measuring rod for Christian service. This urgency does not fade when one enters ministerial ranks; its abiding intensity is sustained until the end of the day. Persons filled with this urgency know there are no shortcuts to the fullness of the stature of Jesus Christ. They are always remembering that "Jesus increased in wisdom and stature, and in favour with God and man" (Luke 2:52).

## The Problem of Biblical Accountability

Now that we have looked at the minister's calling, divine revelation, and maturity, we turn our attention to the use of the Bible. God's Word, the Holy Bible, is the minister's basic text. As a text, the Bible is rather deceptive. While we receive it as a book, we can easily overlook its being a book of many books. Its subject matter covers all known conditions of life, and its pages have something positive to say to those conditions. It is not mastered in a single class, nor are its contents adequately covered in a one- or two-year course.

A lack of understanding this fact has led many ministers to raise the question: If ministers get their sermons from God, why must they spend such long hours preparing them? Why don't they just open their mouths and wait for the Lord to speak through them what he would have them say?[4] This question persists because many persons overlook the Bible as a foundation rule of faith for all human utterances and experiences. Persons asking this question overlook the agonizing struggles, pains, and sorrow often absolutely necessary to receive a meaningful word from the Lord. Job suffered long and hard before he saw God face to face (Job 42:5). Job's experience is a lesson for today's minister who seeks to be relevant and on target.

The problem of biblical accountability can be compared to the driver of a car. If the car is not well tuned and running properly, the engine will sputter and power will be lost. The car is liable to fail even in the midst of rushing traffic. If the preacher is not well tuned and disciplined in matters of faith, he too will go wanting in testing hours. The Bible demands from every student long hours of searching, long voyages into ancient history, deep devotional meditation, study of church history, and sensitivity to the moving presence of God.

If one only had to open one's mouth and God would speak through it, how much poorer we all would be! One would not know the joys, thrills, and excitement of sitting at the feet of great minds, sharing and receiving their studied insights, and being transfixed by the richness of their experiences. One would not be able to walk historic corridors of faith with Abraham, Sarah, Moses, Hagar, David, Hannah, Isaiah, Ruth, Mary, mother of our Lord, and Paul the great apostle. One would not be able literally to wrestle with the Eternal, even as Jacob, and come to mystical truths regarding the nature of

Christ. The cross and all its meaning for human life, the fact of the resurrection, and the eternal nature of the church would not merit the ceaseless concerns scholars know they command today. One would not be acquainted with the divine history of faith, the mighty liberating acts of God in the lives of his people, releasing the captives and setting the prisoners free. One would not know the joy that comes through the disciplined life of study, hard work, and the sublime satisfaction of accomplishment. No workrooms, spiritual tools of faith, or libraries would be needed since only an instant hookup with God would do. This myth needs to be challenged since it contains an element of truth but conveys an even greater element of error!

God can and does speak through his Word directly to his servant, but always in concert with the existential forces of the moment. In times of a patient's serious illness, with a life fluctuating between life and death, the doctor does not have time to go to research books. He or she must diagnose and prescribe quickly! His or her whole training and life's work come to bear on the problem at hand. The minister who has committed one's life to God need not worry. In life's crisis moments, the spirit of God has covenanted to be there to tell his servant exactly what to say! That is the meaning to be gained from the words of Christ: "But when they deliver you up, take no thought how or what ye shall speak: for it shall be given you in that same hour what ye shall speak" (Matthew 10:19). God's word will be there to provide diagnosis and remedy. This is why a life dedicated to the service of Jesus Christ is so important. It pays off when one least expects it. God never fails when the mouthpiece is a trumpet of a life previously grounded in his Word, a soul bathed long hours in devotion, and a body aglow as the holy temple of Almighty God.

When one proclaims, "The Lord has called me to preach," a statement of humanity's finest worth is sounded. It is an utterance that says at once that the Almighty has seen some use for that life and has chosen that person for his service. It affirms God's concern for humanity, God's self-disclosure to humanity, and God's actions in the arena of human life. This chapter has not sought to demean that call, but rather to clarify its nature and urge its recipients to go forth to greater service. It raises the serious questions, "Should I permit God to invest so much in me while I invest so little in him? Should I just take my call, declare my instant revelation, and become overnight an absolute authority in God's Word?" An answer to these questions is already found in the Word of God. "Thou shalt love the Lord thy God with all thy heart, and with all thy soul, and with all thy mind. This is the first and great commandment" (Matthew 22:37-38).

Our attention will next turn to charisma and the whole charismatic involvement of the minister. An attempt will be made to see how images can be manipulated for quick gain, glamour, and passing glory. Only the image of Christ working in and through us can overcome their tempting lure.

# The Charismatic Myth

# 3

The word "charisma" is popularly used these days. We talk about it; we seem to want it; but few, no doubt, understand its subtleties or really know what it entails. It is a word that comes from the Greek word " χαρισματα ," meaning "gifts of grace." It is the divinely endowed blessing given to persons for the due fulfillment of their vocations. In a much narrower sense, it is used to refer to religious leaders who glow with personality and radiate with the presence of God's Spirit.

Persons in our times who believe they have not been fully equipped to do God's will until they have accepted Christ and then received the baptism of the Holy Ghost, with the outward manifestation of speaking in tongues, make up what is known as the charismatic movement. This broad-based grouping of persons, reaching into most major Protestant denominations, and some Roman Catholics, has sought to call the Christian church to accept the fullness of the presence of God in human life. They believe that fullness provides new joy, instant miracles, cures for diseases, powers over nature and even over material objects. They believe persons can now speak in other tongues and produce revealed words of knowledge, as the Spirit of God gives utterance.

The charismatic movement relies heavily on personal testimonies and usually seeks to give a word that authenticates beyond doubt the intervention of God in the matrix of human life. One example was given in a meeting of Full Gospel Businessmen, International, in Baltimore, Maryland. One of the businessmen rose to give his personal testimony. He had been a police officer and had participated in some shady dealings. One night, alone in his car, he was convicted of his sins, and though he had been a practicing Catholic, he was convinced salvation came that night. With his hands lifted up, he found himself speaking in other tongues, praising and glorifying God. In a spiritual daze he rode about that night for about two hours, sorting out what had happened to him, overlooking the fact that his car had no gasoline. Notwithstanding the needle being on empty, he continued his praise until finally the car came to rest at the refueling station, where the engine conked out. This brother has made right the wrongs of his past life and has no doubt now that he is living in the fullness of God's power.

In this chapter, charisma will refer to the characteristics of one person and the possible effects one's life-style and images have upon others. The use of the term "charismatic movement" will focus on the gathering of persons who have been saved from their sins through the shed blood of Jesus, baptized with the Holy Spirit, who speak in other tongues and make use of newly discovered powers inherent in their new relationship with God.

Paul talked about the necessity for spiritual gifts in his letter to Corinth. "But the manifestation of the Spirit is given to every man to profit withal" (1 Corinthians 12:7). Paul enumerated gifts comprising the word of wisdom, the word of knowledge, faith, the gifts of healing, working of miracles, prophecy, discerning of spirits, tongues, and the interpretation of tongues. The charisma of service, stated Paul, was found in apostles, prophets, teachers, and those entrusted with the government of the church.

There exists the danger that the Christian minister might study and cultivate those images that project to others a holy and reverent personality that is not genuinely real. One might project an image to others just to impress and magnetize others under the scope of one's own powers. Here is the chief danger facing the one blessed with charisma. One will certainly need influence in the ministry. One will need a personality that attracts those whom one leads. Still one must labor long and hard to see that others see the living Christ in one's words and actions, or double exposures of one's images will surface in the minds of the people.

## The Spirit-Filled Image

When the apostle Paul penned the words "... but our sufficiency is of God; who also hath made us able ministers of the new testament: not of the letter, but of the spirit: for the letter killeth, but the spirit giveth life" (2 Corinthians 3:5-6), he gave opportunity for many minds to seize his words out of context and to argue the uselessness of the letter and the absolute totality of the spirit. It matters not that Paul was seeking to drive home his utter sincerity as a gospel preacher, his denial of self, and his commendation of the people of God, the Body of Christ. We seldom hear this explanation when these words are quoted. Many ministerial minds are led to believe "if we can be filled simply with the Holy Ghost, we can be popular and powerful with God."

For this reason alone, it would be a good thing if seminaries placed a greater emphasis on the systematic study of the Holy Spirit as seen in the Bible and the history of the church. I went through seminary and had spent several years in the ministry before I undertook to study the Holy Spirit as a Person of God, in the pursuit of a doctor's degree at St. Mary's Ecumenical Seminary, Baltimore, Maryland. I had gone to seminary with a general understanding of God's triune nature. I believed in God as Father of all life, Redeemer of humankind in the Person of Jesus Christ his Son, and Comforter of life in the Person of the Holy Spirit. In seminary, I found that most of the theological emphasis was given to God the Father and God the Son. A noticeable absence of study was given to God as Holy Spirit. Perhaps it was assumed that one would gain a deeper knowledge of God's Spirit in the arena of life. No doubt this is one of the reasons so much confusion has existed over the doctrine of the Holy Spirit. Too long has a thorough systematic study of God's spiritual presence been left to chance.

Only in the directed study of God the Holy Spirit did I fully see and appreciate the unfolding and developing concept of the Spirit of God as revealed in Old and New Testament teachings. Every ministerial student would do well to see God's Spirit at work in the Old Testament, imparting strength, knowledge, and wisdom. This foundation of truth would provide a deeper understanding of Jesus' relationship with his Father as One. There would be no Pentecost, no early New Testament church movement, no revolutionary preaching of the gospel without the absolute belief and power of the Holy Ghost. I believe the same Person of the Holy Ghost is fully alive and available now to empower present-day disciples in the church.

This available power can carry the minister beyond surface charismatic traits of joy, happiness, and continued holy enthusiasm. One can go beyond the need to impress others that one has contact with God. Walking and talking with holier-than-thou attitudes would become meaningless. Ideas of being God's special humanity would be given up for the solid ministry of servanthood and stewardship of Christ. No longer would we have to speak with holy tones from pulpit or marketplace. Gazing mystical eyes, as though looking into the very presence of God, would no longer be part of one's act. One would not practice those traits until one became hypnotized by them. In time all traits practiced long enough can become false foundations. Then in moments when the people are no longer present, when the organ is silent, one broods in self-despondency because something in one cries out against the conflict raging in one's life.

One of the pitfalls of the self-sustained, Spirit-filled image is the denial of the rhythmic rising and falling emotional patterns of life. No one can stay on mountain experiences all the time. Life has low moments when burdens press down, and energy wanes.

> There are times we feel moody regardless of how much we believe in the power of God or would like to be more like Jesus in our hearts, as we were told we should be in Sunday school. If we are not to fake a good mood or pretend we never have spells of moodiness, what are we to do?
> My thesis is this: Moodiness is the result of trying to play God.[1]

That is exactly what the minister is not called to do. No one plays God without catastrophe. One can only represent, speak for, and live for God.

Congregations can generally discern a real person from a pretender. Those incessant day-by-day problems, fraught with seen and unseen difficulties, have ways of forcing the true personality of the minister to the surface, even when one is not aware of it. To assume that the projected spirit-filled life is a genuine substitute for the Christlike life is really a violent disservice to the gospel of Jesus Christ. It places trust more in self than in Christ. It enthrones self as god to be admired and worshiped. It eliminates the need for Christ to call us out of our broken, fallen nature and restore us whole and fit for his kingdom. There is no need to surrender our past lives and lay hold of the grace of God we have in the Body of Christ.

A spirit-filled life that is devoid of rigorous theological beliefs is prone to dangerous consequences in so many ways. Paul dealt with the schism in the church at Corinth. Some of its members wanted to use piety as a leverage over less pious and spirit-filled members. Paul rebuked those members who wanted simply to make an end out of mere spiritual manifestations:

> What is it then? I will pray with the spirit, and I will pray with the understanding also: I will sing with the spirit, and I will sing with the understanding also. Else when thou shalt bless with the spirit, how shall he that occupieth the room of the unlearned say Amen at thy giving of thanks, seeing he understandeth not what thou sayest? (1 Corinthians 14:15-16).

Paul did not want to see religious ceremony and practice degenerate into sounds without substance, actions without direction. He wanted all things done in the church aimed at edifying members in the Body of Christ. Paul knew that an underlying Christian theology was vitally necessary for the Christian faith.

"One of the most surprising weaknesses of the Christian ministry in the recent past has been the neglect of rigorous theology. Preachers, assuming what they had no right to assume, have dealt in their sermons with peripheral topics, without realizing that many of the members are lacking in the fundamentals."[2] A keen understanding of the way of God reveals that spiritual power is intimately related to a thorough knowledge of the Word of God. That word has a built-in law, logic, and purpose that must be understood and never violated. That word, in the light of Hebrew understanding, is the carrier of its own inherent powers! Somehow God's spirit is still related to the appreciation and application of his Holy Word to the problems of life. Paul's admonition that spiritual power must be balanced by its merit to communicate, to edify, and to promote the work of Christ remains the final test of the spirit-filled life.

In New Shiloh Baptist Church, Baltimore, Maryland, following a morning's message, seven adults presented themselves for membership in the congregation. A man, approximately forty-five years of age, rushed forward to speak to the minister, "Reverend, I need your help. I want to be filled with the Holy Spirit. I want the baptism!" I responded to the brother with the following words: "Sir, you are looking for God to blow his spirit on you, as air fills a balloon. God can fill you this way, but never does without surrender. God's spirit usually fills us through accepting Christ, receiving and living his word, and sharing fellowship with his church. It is in the fellowship of the Body of Christ that we are filled!"

The Reverend C. David Matthews, minister of the First Baptist Church, Greenville, South Carolina, spoke to the same problem:

> In many of our Baptist churches, pastors succeed only through promising and pushing the highly questionable opiate of religious experience. And the quantitative success of many of these churches may be more an evidence of a deep cultural sickness than a testimony to the validity of the gospel. . . . A so-called Christian experience can feed our narcissism and develop in us a sense of self-righteousness. In other words, one's love for one's experience can be a subtle form of loving oneself. The calling of God, biblically, is not so much the occasion of ecstatic experiences as it is the occasion of moral demands.[3]

The Reverend Matthews calls attention to an area of overlooked concerns of both the one who seeks to be charismatic as well as the charismatic movement as a whole. Even if one fulfilled all one's holy vows and had received miraculous powers from God, the question of moral concerns remains. One of the first questions raised in Old Testament life is still there, "Am I my brother's keeper?" (Genesis 4:9). The apostle Paul spoke about many so-called spirit-filled lives in the church at Corinth. Still, their names are not given. We know nothing about their redemptive labors of love. We do know that Paul, who preferred knowledge and edification to meaningless piety and misdirected holiness, was used by Christ to bridge the gospel from East to West, from Jew to Gentile, from words about Christ to a theology of Christ.

## The Bible-Quoting Image

Not every one that saith unto me, Lord, Lord, shall enter into the kingdom of heaven; but he that doeth the will of my Father which is in heaven. Many will say to me in that day, Lord, Lord, have we not prophesied in thy name? and in thy name have cast out devils? and in thy name done many wonderful works? And then I will profess unto them, I never knew you: depart from me, ye that work iniquity (Matthew 7:21-23).

Jesus identified Bible quoting as a potential hazard to effective ministry. Jesus knew some would use God's name for selfish purposes, to build up their own kingdoms. Jesus even implied that many would work the astounding miracle of casting out devils, appearing to others as live agents in the ministry of Christ. Beyond miracle works, many Bible quoters would do "wonderful works." It does not take a lot of profound thought to imagine what power one today would command if the world exalted one's works as wonderful. Even though today we have so many conveniences, programs, systems of living, and cultural accomplishments, some minister could still impress others by doing wonderful things. Jesus wrote them all off with one conclusion, "I never knew you!"

The Bible, the minister's basic text and one's final source of authority in all matters of faith, is the one book one ought really to know. There is a difference between knowledge and the open display of knowledge. Doing God's work and saving lost souls do not require a display of memorized proof texts so much as the guiding ministry of God's Spirit. The best medical doctors prescribe only a limited amount of medicine per dose for the patient. God's Word is also effectively received, ". . . precept upon precept; line upon line, line upon line; here a little, and there a little" (Isaiah 28:10).

Part of our problem lies in the question of whether there is power in quoting the Bible even though the people may not understand what is being said. To the extent that people do have a special reverence for the Bible, a special place in their hearts for its contents, the first answer to this problem would be "yes." But that is not the whole story. Revelation without human application is sterile and meaningless. People hear and agree to a lot of words they do not fully accept and understand. Americans sing that this land is the "land of the free and the home of the brave." However, working out avenues for the freedom of all her peoples continues to try the souls of the warriors of justice and love, while others keep living and care less. Getting congregations to apply just one relevant text to life may demand greater leadership than quoting many texts and applying none.

A study of the epic events of the Old Testament reveals that each generation must rediscover God for itself. The great acts of the Old Testament—the creation, the Exodus, covenant, the Exile, building and dedication of the temple—were all acts of faith for Israel that come alive only as they are relived in the now. Indeed the whole Bible must come alive for every generation, or else the Bible will rest as any other book, collecting dust on some forgotten shelf.

Quoting Scriptures is vastly different from causing Scriptures to come alive and illumine some contemporary problem. Quoting Scriptures without serious application to events at hand can be cold, callous, a kind of intellectual display of biblical knowledge. It tends to promote a kind of biblical blasphemy, or the worship of the Bible itself. Scripture should be that Word of God that moves the minister beyond showy, judgmental, and dramatic impressions upon others. The one who stands declaring God's words always remembers that in time some other may use the same method upon one's ministry and work.

I believe Jesus called attention to the emptiness of Bible quotations because his doctrine of the kingdom always tied the life of one to another. Serving God demands the bearing of fruit. "Some form of social gospel is required if each man is recognized as being the object of God's care, and if, consequently, each is his brother's brother."[4] Every minister will be judged by the words of our Lord, "And why call ye me, Lord, Lord, and do not the things which I say?" (Luke 6:46).

James, an apostle of our Lord, wrestled with this problem and concluded, "Even so faith, if it hath not works, is dead, being alone. . . . Thou believest that there is one God; thou doest well: the devils also believe, and tremble" (James 2:17, 19). James's balance of faith and works is all the more important in our present pragmatic age. Men and women need to see evidences of the changed lives of Christian disciples, with a concerned ministry to the poor, food for the hungry, hope and renewed life for the prisonbound. Only then will the word become flesh anew and dwell in the hearts and lives of persons.

There is a story about a certain pastor who preached a certain message to his flock. Sunday after Sunday he preached the same text, "Love ye one another." Finally the church got fed up and agreed someone should speak to the pastor. The head deacon approached the pastor and said, "Reverend, I have come to see if you might preach to us some new text from the Bible. We are all wearied with the same one." The pastor responded, "When you brothers and sisters decide to really love one another in Christ, I'll move on to another text."

There is a sense in which the minister is blessed if one can drive home one great gospel truth into the hearts of the hearers in a twelve-month span. One does not quickly come to understand and receive the deep truths of God's Word. Really to see and know that God's Word is real takes time, study, repetition, and living experiences. Preaching one text is no pattern to be followed, but it does show the difficult job found in moving people's lives closer to the Master. Biblical variety is an invaluable source for growth and Christlike fulfillment.

When the Word becomes flesh and dwells in the minister, people will respond to Christ because they see the servant of Christ. When the Word becomes flesh and dwells in the minister, God's servant becomes a living shepherd feeding people through actions, deeds of love, intercession for human weaknesses, and the discovery of powers people never knew they had. When the Word becomes flesh in the minister, one rises above the myth of bibliolatry and says "no" to the pitfalls of seeking to use God's Word for selfish purposes and hidden crutches. Instead one lives out one's life as a modern-day version of the ever-living story.

## The Scholarship Myth

A great pressure is upon the theologically trained minister to convey to the congregation an image of attained scholarship. The minister feels the pressure to speak with authority. One has to have theological positions for all of one's utterances. One is under pressure to come off as a liberal, or a fundamentalist, or sometimes as a basic Bible-believing conservative. Going through the mind of the minister is the question, "How can I get the people to know that I know what I am talking about and am not shooting from the hip?" Since effectiveness with the people is largely determined by verbal communication, the minister wants to come through as a power in his class. In one's efforts to make a particular impression, it is possible to stifle the creative flow that ought to be a part of normal ministerial and congregational development as a team.

The late Dr. J. Pius Barbour, minister of Calvary Baptist Church, Chester, Pennsylvania, often instructed seminarians, who frequently visited his home, with these words: "In developing your theological and hermeneutical minds, learn to read a text and exegete it in your own minds, thoroughly flushing it through your own experiences. Stay away from biblical commentaries until you have done some independent research and given your spirits a chance for creative thought." Dr. Barbour's experience as a theologian and preacher had informed him of the dangers of total reliance on others for theological and biblical authority. He wanted each minister to be able to say honestly, "This I see in the Word of God."

The minister who constantly parades before hearers the names of scholars who said this or that runs the danger of diminishing the authority rightly earned through one's call and subsequent preparation. Working through this problem is not easy. Consider for a moment that when one studies the great sayings of Jesus, almost all of them are given in simple everyday words, conveying messages about life's most complex subjects in easy to understand fashion. The words of Jesus, the central figure of our faith, contrast sharply with the language of theology, church history, and moral philosophies one has studied in seminary. To speak in the language of Jesus obviously makes more sense but may not adequately reveal to others the literary disciplines gained along the way. The test of time provides us with the clue to our answer. Theologies about God live and die, depending upon their abilities to communicate some truth. The so-called simple words of Jesus are eternally precise because they communicate God's truth to every age and to all classes of persons.

Every minister should discover one's soul and natural style of preaching. Some have the abilities to quote others at length and then amplify their words. Others are poetic in style and content, revealing Christ in shades of flashing beauty. Still others are theological and highly systematic, driving home eternal truths. There remains still another group of exhortative and prophetic preachers, who move congregations to redress social evils and set captive persons free. Each minister must find one's own creative preaching niche and develop that niche to its height for the glory of God.

The minister is a part of all the influences that have come upon one's life, good and bad. Great minds that have illumined the minister's spirit must not be discarded. They are part of the ongoing stream of Christian revitalization. By nature of the minister's calling, one becomes a part of the apostolic succession. Others have gone before. Others will follow. The minister has a rightful duty to pay homage to those spiritual warriors. It would be the rankest kind of plagiarism not to acknowledge one's source of learning and enrichment. Those whom one quotes ought to illumine one's hearers in the truths of the faith and help to communicate the good news of God's Word.

The minister is a public person and cannot escape some pull of the entertainment syndrome. However, the minister can consciously decide whether to be an intellectual showperson or an arouser of conviction. There is a sense in which people want to be entertained in every facet of life in today's world. Radio, television, sports, and modern America's general life-style beg for more and more entertainment. The church has a moral responsibility to go beyond the shallowness of entertainment and feed persons on the Word of God. Paraded scholarship without Christ is like "sounding brass or a tinkling cymbal"! Intellectual integrity ought to equip the preacher to communicate better the fundamental truths of the faith, especially in a time when there is a revival of born-again experiences but little attention is given to the moral and social responsibilities attendant to those who accept Christ as Savior.

Genuine biblical scholarship loses itself in its search for God. It seeks not to parade the letter but seeks to exalt the central personality of our faith. Is Christ the supreme revelation of God in our present world of many competing gods? Who is Jesus Christ? What is his purpose for humankind? How do we relate to his spirit in the world today? What is the purpose of his church and where is it going? Are we creatures only of time? Does death end all? These are not easy questions, and they will always engage creative, thinking minds. When God's servants use their abilities to help people to deal positively with these questions and find meaning for life, then living both for ministers and for people is not in vain.

In the end, charisma is more than what we do, what we say, the way we act or speak, and the way we hold our hands. Charisma is more than being called to preach, trafficking in holy things, be they Bible, crucifixes, or holy vestments. Charisma is more than our acquired personalities and our intellectual attainments. Real charisma is who we are and not what we are.

We are indebted to the charismatic movement in our times for bringing us renewed attention to the reality of God as Holy Ghost. Our sense of personal witness has been strengthened by this movement's attention to the immediate powers of God for human life. Still we see dangers in spirit-filled lives that fail to see their sisters and brothers and reach out to them with healing hands. We see dangers in any movement that ends up separating one branch of Zion from another under false assumptions of spiritual superiority. Only God knows and can finally try the hearts and lives of persons.

The slave once sang, "I've got shoes, you got shoes, all a God's chillun got shoes!" That same message could be applied to charismatics: "I've got charisma; you've got charisma; all a God's chillun got charisma!" As we develop our natural and spiritual selves to their fullest capacities, we see the strength and the impact God's grace produces upon our lives. Forcing this gift on others is a spiritual mockery. To be our finer selves, in his service, enhances this grace to the glory of God.

Our study will now focus on charisma as it seeks to work on our lower selves. Charisma not only seeks to glow in the pulpit, but it also arouses the erotic nature in persons. The concupiscence myth will be our next subject.

# The Concupiscence Myth

# 4

. . . ordain elders in every city, as I had appointed thee: If any be blameless, the husband of one wife, having faithful children not accused of riot or unruly. For a bishop must be blameless, as the steward of God, not selfwilled, not soon angry, not given to wine, no striker, not given to filthy lucre. But a lover of hospitality, a lover of good men, sober, just, holy, temperate (Titus 1:5-7).

The tone set in the preceding passage demands spiritual excellence. Indeed, the Christian ministry demands the best from one's being. It is a full-time calling. Seven days a week, day and night, the minister is conveying some sort of image to others. The minister is under pressure to adopt images, real or imagined, others expect from this work. The minister desires to be accepted, to belong, to be a part of the people, to be thought of as affable and a regular person. This need for recognition and acceptance can lead the minister to acts and behaviorisms not representative of one's Christian calling. It can even lead to concupiscence.

In moral theology, concupiscence is that desire for temporal ends which has its seat in the senses. Paul talked about that desire in his letter to the Romans. "But sin, taking occasion by the commandment, wrought in me all manner of concupiscence. For without the

law sin was dead" (Romans 7:8). It was the theologian who taught
that the cause of concupiscence was humanity's fall in Adam who
transmitted a depraved nature to all persons, where the desires of the
flesh seek to control the reason of the spirit. Concupiscence occurs
when the higher faculties of human life are subordinated to the lustful
desires of the flesh. Satisfying this desire places the minister on an
endless road where the light of reason and faith constantly diminish.

The glorification of the concupiscence myth is as old as stories
surrounding the legendary activities of Adam and Eve and as current
as the pastor, fresh out of seminary, seeking to prove the virility of
self. The passions of human flesh create a potential for controlling all
persons, including the Christian minister. In the natural order of
things, man is attracted to woman and woman is attracted to man.
This attraction is expressed in thousands of ways. It is sometimes
expressed through the fashion of clothes. It breaks through in
language, facial expressions, and bodily characteristics. Almost every
dealing with humanity has the potential for some sexual involvement.
Coping with this known and obvious fact should not be left to chance
in the development of ministerial character.

Since sex presents such a formidable problem in ministerial ranks,
an in-depth study of its impact on this calling would be a blessing in
seminary circles. Seminary would be a good place to deal with the
nuts and bolts of human interactions and how the minister might
serve others effectively without being the passive or active victim of
those one serves. One way seminaries can approach this issue is to call
for radical obedience to the love ethic of Jesus Christ. The Scripture
has already called for a blameless ministry. The experienced pastor
knows there is a big gap between those profound words and the
realities of life. While seminarians write lofty papers on "The Nature
of Man," "The Nature of Sin," "The Problem of Guilt," "The Nature
of the Church," and the like, many of the basic everyday problems of
the flesh versus the spirit go wanting.

In this last quarter of the twentieth century, when Watergate
history and subsequent revelations have forced American legislators
to reexamine their duties and set new ethical standards for their
profession, can the servants of God do any less than come to grips
with the realized and potential problems of their own humanity? The
minister's humanity cannot be permanently hidden behind the cloth,

the cloak, or the pulpit. The minister needs counsel, guidance, pastoring, and moral support. Support comes only when problems are identified and dealt with honestly.

The moral crisis of the present age cannot be dealt with apart from ministerial involvement. It would be foolish to assume that the Christian ministry is totally above the immoral decadence of our day. Before God, the ministry must be held responsible, at least in part, for much of the moral crisis of our times. Christian ministers are the heralders of truth. They are supposed to be the conscience of the communities they serve. They are suffering servants of the people and are inextricably bound up in the lives of the people.

The greatest revival needed in present-day American life is a revival of morality based upon the love ethics of Jesus Christ. This revival will not claim the popularity the "born again" boom has claimed, but it will have far more redeeming effects. This revival is a distinct possibility in our times, since the Christian faith has shown a historic ability to renew itself and to produce ministers who lift up high standards for the people to follow.

A thorough indoctrination of the moral integrity a minister ought to possess would help send forth soldiers of righteousness against the ungodliness of this age. Rampant pornographic books fill the newsstands telling the casual reader that happiness is found in free sex. Permissive philosophies, such as "doing one's thing," have lowered the high call of ethical duty. Fervent and religious-like devotion paid to sports heroes has all but eclipsed serious attention given to the lives of those in Christian faith and community service. Christian education has often become too separated from basic Bible doctrines, leaving the pupils with a God made in the image of humankind, and not the sovereign God of the Bible, known but unknown to persons. In this kind of world, the minister needs to establish oneself as a leader of moral powers! When this responsibility to justice, love, and righteousness is neglected, all the people suffer. Senior ministers must be especially concerned about the kind of influence their lives are exerting in shaping the lives of younger ministers aspiring to be ambassadors of God.

## From Generation to Generation

The overwhelming burden of the ministry is such that younger ministers almost instinctively attach themselves to older ministers, to study their ways, possibly to catch their spirit, and to learn as much about their calling as possible. They see the older minister as a kind of godfather, one who has gone up through the ranks and arrived intact. This minister is living proof of what God can do with the broken pieces of human life. By the younger minister's studying and becoming a spiritual part of the senior minister, the strengths and weaknesses of that ministry are passed along, from generation to generation. The influence of the minister seen as master by his pupil is exceedingly powerful and can shape one's life indefinitely.

While talking with seminarians in his home J. Pius Barbour often counseled these young theologians with these words: "The minister should be constantly on guard against three major pitfalls: loose women, liquor, and accountability with money. Don't get yourself involved in prestige fights! Why fight about who's the boss of the church when God has made you preacher and pastor! But above all that, the worst sin is not to preach!" Barbour had that rare ability to rap with theological students at the level of their own concerns, bringing to their questions his studied scholarship and grass-roots wisdom. He permitted his own humanity to enter his conversations, permitting the student to see the man behind the cloth. How vastly different he was from many ministers who have refused to be honest and have sought to veil themselves with unreal personalities!

In an attempt to justify some ministerial illicit sexual behavior, some ministers have argued that the calling makes their work public, and so the profession must relate to all the people. Was not David a public man and didn't he relate to whom he pleased? The minister's nomadic and itinerant schedule is a factor that must be considered in one's life-style. What is more, adultery in Scripture is a spiritual problem, bringing about estrangement between people and God. It does not refer to one's sexual behavior! All these and other arguments have been used to justify human weakness in ministerial ranks. Some have tried to see illicit sexual relationships as a means of using leverage for survival and well-being among the people. At points, some ministers have boasted about their profligacy in sexual matters, causing younger ministers to feel that satisfying bodily passions is one of the hidden blessings of this fellowship.

Today's seminaries need to bring the question of sexual behavior out of the closet and discuss its glory and its despair, its fulfillment and its destructive forces, in the light of calm, sound, rational judgment. This needs to be done because the mass media has often painted an unreal picture of the church and the ministry of Jesus Christ. A few years ago, it was Flip Wilson, the comedian, and his church of What's Happening Now! making overt appeals to the sisters. The viewing American public always knew there was an overtone of sex and material greed in that portrayal. More recently, the movie *Which Way Is Up?,* starring Richard Pryor, has also made use of a church scene. The pastor is seen as a ladies' man while the pastor's wife is seduced and ridiculed!

We have always been able to say and dramatize in theater the acts that would not be communicated otherwise. The fact that some comedians have chosen the church and its ministry as source material for their jokes presents a problem that will not soon go away. No one minister is called to hold up the profession of the whole, but each one is called to be faithful before God. Even enemies can call attention to our problems, our weak spots. Perhaps the Christian ministry has failed to reveal a leadership of moral and spiritual authority that will make the Flip Wilsons and Richard Pryors turn elsewhere. Their messages to us point up a need to be morally strong and spiritually vigilant in the faith, lest vile temptations overcome us.

In the Old Testament, Elijah left us a picture of leaving the substance of his ministry upon his youthful follower, Elisha. In the moment of his earthly transition, Elisha wanted to see the relevant utterances of God's words and the championing of righteous causes continued. It was inconceivable to this young prophet that such a powerful ministry should perish with the departure of the saint. "And it came to pass, when they were gone over, that Elijah said unto Elisha, Ask what I shall do for thee, before I am taken away from thee. And Elisha said, I pray thee, let a double portion of thy spirit be upon me" (2 Kings 2:9). Elisha's request was notable for what it did not say. No material gains or worldly powers were requested from the elder generation by the younger generation! Persons do not automatically seek the higher and finer things of life. The spirit-filled ministry of Elijah had awakened in those about him a desire for life's higher blessings. A positive ministry of righteousness can still awaken in persons instincts and realities of their higher selves before God.

President Jimmy Carter came to the office of the presidency of the United States on a campaign that spoke to the moral needs of our day. In his many campaign speeches, he promised a return of emphasis to the Christian family. He called for old-fashioned patriotism, based upon a love of God and country. He openly promised to be a president of all the people, with particular attention given to those caught in historic vices of poverty, racism, and class barriers. He proclaimed publicly that he had experienced the new birth in Christ and that he found time to teach Sunday school lessons in his Baptist church.

In a news broadcast televised nationally June 30, 1977, the following question was put to the president: "Mr. President, do you expect those working in your cabinet and administration to have monogamous relationships, and what action will you take to those who fail to do so?" The president responded, "Well, my relationship is certainly monogamous, and I could wish others likewise. To those who have fallen from grace, well, I'll pray for them." When this kind of discussion is openly engaged in, in the halls of government, its fallout is bound to have some impact on the citizenry.

The pluralism of religions now openly competing in the American marketplace has placed an even greater burden upon Christianity to show itself as a faith of the strongest moral and social power. It is the contention of this book that Christianity is not just another faith among many faiths, but that it is the supreme and final revelation of God for humankind in the person of Jesus Christ. There is no finer love ethic and way of life than that found in the teachings and example of Jesus. Notwithstanding, life does not grant any faith strength without struggle, power without challenge, and movement without opposition. The Christian church and its seminaries must not be lulled to sleep by the glorious Christian past, bequeathed through blood and tears. Each generation of Christians must pass to the next a righteously moral torch held high above the multicolored hues of a neon-lighted world. Passing along the torch of moral purity and exemplary sexual behavior from one generation to another calls for a willingness to commit oneself totally to the Christian ministry without fear of life or the loss of some vital narcissistic pleasure.

When the minister has this kind of commitment and dedication to Christ, one's service to others becomes free and creative. Counseling couples and leading them in marriage vows is satisfying. Blessing newborn babies and leading parents in the offering of their lives to Christ is rewarding. No risk of emotional involvement develops in times of counseling others with marital stresses and financial disasters. One's voice is heard in the sickroom, at the graveside, laying departed ones to rest. One's weekly sermons are already reinforced by a life of solid commitment to the way of the cross. One is above seizing the normal, natural adulation of one's ministry, generously received from others as an opportunity for self-serving gains.

All of this will demand a reawakened ministry to moral righteousness that surpasses the moral attitudes of our day. A whole period of breakdown of family, social, educational, and governmental standards has swept our American culture. Some churches, responding to this new way of life, discontinued traditional Bible teachings based upon Mosaic laws, "thou shalt nots," in favor of new ethical teachings flexible for situations, circumstances, and personalities. The results have been a loss of the fear of God and a loose acceptance of the ways of humanity.

This need not be. A cadre of baptized believers in the Body of Christ, championed by a dedicated ministry, can lead the modern world to new spiritual victories and triumphs over demonic sins. The same God who sent Jeremiah through the streets of ancient Jerusalem looking for a man is still searching the hearts of his servants, looking for disciples who will sell out and live for him.

## From Festive Conventions to Lost Convictions

The Christian ministry has always turned to occasional meetings to keep faith alive, to share vital fellowship, and to project basic positions of faith. The early councils of the church gathered together ever so often to speak as one on subjects such as Belief in God, The Nature of Christ, The Nature of Church, The Nature of Man, The World and Eschatology. Our emphasis is not to question church persons' needs for conventions, but rather to raise some serious questions as to whether basic needs are being met through conventions today. Are we keeping in focus the purpose of our being, the nature of our calling? Is the Lord's work being done when we gather in hotels and motels so entertainment orientated that the voice of Christ is barely heard? Here are some of the facts.

First, the traditional impact clergy have had on everyday people during conventional gatherings is a thing of the past. Usually, modern-day hotels, motels, and convention centers are located downtown or in some luxuriously manicured vacation spot. Going to these places affords many poor persons the opportunity for exposure to some of life's plush experiences as paid delegates of their churches. While this is being done, however, Christian missions are often blurred. The gospel messages that should stir the city and call persons to commit their lives to Christ are usually lost behind walls of inns and hotels. There is a legitimate ministry of travel and cultural exposure in which the church ought to engage. However, to do so under the banner of conventions leaves Christian stewardship wanting. Thousands of dollars spent in travel and lodging do not seem to justify the small amount of money given to advance the work of the kingdom of God. I suspect every minister has silently wondered about this kind of stewardship in the sight of God. The airlines, hotels, and taxis get the money while the work of Christ gets the non-budgeted tips.

Second, for many ministers, convention time has become a time for relaxation and play. It is that one time of the year when the brothers and sisters can get together without the restrictive bonds of familiar community and city life. One can be freer and enjoy many of the things of life not experienced at other times. This attitude enhanced by holiday settings makes doing the Lord's work next to impossible.

Dr. Thomas Kilgore, president of the Progressive National Baptist Convention, had this to say in his address to that body:

> We are duty bound to be good stewards of the resources that our churches give us to attend the convention. They give us time away from our regular duties, and they give us money to take care of our Christian needs. It is not fair—and it may be extortion—to accept church financing to come to the convention, and then spend a significant portion of your time outside of the sessions. My brothers and sisters, if your church sends you here as a delegate, it is not fair for you to use your money and time for a semi-vacation. We need you in each session—on time and for the whole time.[1]

Dr. Kilgore sought to move the delegates from a tradition of levity at convention times that has gained a strong hold on many. There is some justification for this attitude. Years past, when travel was not so frequent, annual meetings of messengers were times of great excitement, festive spirits, renewal, and relaxation. Just to attend the meetings and be with the fellowship had tremendous ongoing value. Much of that climate has changed today.

Coast to coast highways and fast jet airplanes have made travel an experience for the masses. The love of going to distant cities and seeing new sights cannot justify calling God's people together. There must be a depth of witness, service, evangelism, and stewardship during times of conventions that make them relevant, purposeful, and directed.

Young ministers, attending conventions for the first time, are strongly influenced by those whom they observe. If others go sightseeing, bathe in pools, lie on beaches, or go out on shopping sprees, these young ministers will get a warped idea of ministry. The fires of dedication will be subdued while the joys of flesh are turned on.

The same pressure for the life of ease often generated at convention times could be transformed to produce a life of profound dedication and service. Perhaps what is needed is a restructuring of the convention concept. Why not have a massive outdoor or indoor rally somewhere in the city to tell the town, "Christians are here!"? The convention could organize well in advance to hold youth meetings which would leave lasting impressions upon the lives of today's generation. Factories and industries located near convention sites could be visited with lasting effect. Parades to witness to the faith could be well planned to seize public attention and openly declare commitment to Jesus Christ, Son of God. All of these suggestions would not be done in any single convention session, but possibilities for impacting the city with a witness for Christ are legend and must not go wanting. The attention of persons today is gained by a unified group that has human concern and redeeming values as primary concerns. The lost world must know the Christian minister is serious about Jesus and believes absolutely that Christ is the answer to human needs.

A new and higher sense of joy and fellowship could be gained making use of innovative programs. It could be that many go to beaches, take shopping trips, and loll about in the halls because substantive Christian matters have not been properly planned to recruit and engage minds and bodies. In times of war, soldiers do not have the luxury of standing around and relaxing with ease. Confronting the enemy requires full-time attention and aggressive behavior. Christian ministers are spiritual soldiers and must behave with studied behavior that reflects discipline and power.

One of the major events in the life of Jesus occurred at festival time in ancient Jerusalem. The time of Passover was the Hebrews' way of remembering their bondage in Egypt and their deliverance by a mighty act of God. Yet across the years, that great festival had grown to be a time of buying and selling, and the gathering of material gains. The original purpose of celebrating and renewing faith was lost in the ring and zing of coins and exchange. Jesus said, "Take these things hence; make not my Father's house an house of merchandise" (John 2:16). "It is written, My house shall be called the house of prayer; but ye have made it a den of thieves" (Matthew 21:13). Jesus intended for the Passover observance to go on, but minus the worldly practices that overshadowed it.

Strong ministers of today must march into festive conventions and set priorities in order. Many practices that do not serve God's kingdom must be cleaned out, so that convictions will not be lost and the cause of Christ made to suffer.

## Popularity Versus Power

One of the inherent dangers of organized religion is its need for popular attention. The organized church, in an effort to promote its being, often resorts to practices that are non-Christian. N. W. Norwood, noted pastor and evangelist of Fairfield, Alabama, stated these words: "Without doubt, Satan will make a man do anything to keep his kingdom going. One of the temptations Satan uses is sex, perhaps the most subtle danger of organized religion. The devil tells him, use this woman, it's done anyway. Perpetuate your kingdom."[2] Once this kind of activity is begun, the door is opened for other activities that quickly compromise ministerial powers. Moneys are subject to be mishandled. Saints are bewildered while ruthless characters seek to run the show. Satan enthrones himself in the hearts of good people on the premise that he can deliver to them the kingdoms they desire.

Overcoming this problem demands a sound Bible teaching

program. In such a program the wise minister would deal candidly with great Bible giants, revealing their strengths and weaknesses, and showing how their lives might bless us today. In this program the minister would exalt Christ through teachings and show how he is the foundation stone for every believer. Another objective of this program would be to show that the clean, godly life is the universal duty of every Christian. No one is exempt from the moral surrender to Christ which is the heart of Christian dogma.

Students would see that their lives are ultimately answerable only to God. The minister's instruction would cover many things. A base of moral authority would be established upon the Word of God. Students would see God's servant as a moral proponent of the teachings expounded. A collective body of committed soldiers would be established to give indepth power for the workings of God's people. Only then can the minister escape the lashing criticism Isaiah leveled upon God's servants centuries ago:

> His watchmen are blind: they are all ignorant; they are all dumb dogs, they cannot bark; sleeping, lying down, loving to slumber. Yea, they are greedy dogs which can never have enough, and they are shepherds that cannot understand: they all look to their own way, every one for his gain, from his quarter (Isaiah 56:10-11).

Once while I was conducting an evangelistic service, I was approached by a minister with the proposal that I buy into an economic plan based upon the pyramid concept. I was assured that my initial $2,000 deposit would make me a partner in the scheme, and every member joining under me would automatically accrue to my account $500. My decision not to join was quickly indicated. Some months later, this Florida-based company was hauled into court and charged with defrauding the public trust and using the mail for malicious purposes. All kinds of get-rich-quick schemes await those who permit their lives to be blown by winds promising big financial success. Now that many states have begun legalized gambling with daily lotteries constantly begging to be played, surely there must be a word from the Lord.

*Time* magazine in its December 6, 1976, issue had a long article entitled "Gambling Goes Legit." The article told the story of how many church people expect to strike rich jackpots in bingo games operated by some churches in New York City. "Today, according to the report of the National Gambling Commission, an overwhelming majority of Americans (more than 80%) regard gambling as an acceptable activity."[3]

*Jet* magazine told the story of a minister who claimed he prayed for the right number and won $56,000. This kind of adverse publicity, associating God with illicit chance, will not edify or build up God's people. Popular fads and mass false expectations deteriorate the moral fiber of persons today who are unaware. When persons awaken to examine lost dreams and shattered lives, they discover a quagmire of broken hopes and worthless gods. Popular get-rich-quick schemes violate the providential nature of God who loves nothing better than providing for and watching over his own.

The more society moves toward complete secularization, the less it depends upon God. Edward C. Devereux, Jr., of Cornell University, had these words to say: "Our society is moving more and more toward secularization, to rationalization, to the collapse of real commitment to public morality. Gambling fits into our whole Machiavellian rationale that anything goes if it works."[4] This is also the philosophy used by ministers seeking fame and popularity. Their argument is, "If it works and draws the people, use it!" Use popular personalities, politicians, leaders, sport stars, whether they be Christian or not; use them if they will draw people. Use them if they will help you get your name before the public. This teaching always causes the one who believes it the loss of moral power that will be needed in the drama of life. The minister should be the ethical and moral ambassador to a world bereft of righteous life. The need for a prophetic ministry, discerning enough to judge morally the sodomic spirit of modern America, is past due. A ministry of public consensus and private accommodation will not do. The church is stronger than secular society. Its message of deliverance for all persons must ring above the disco sounds of this rock-freak age and provide eternal guidance in the wilderness of life's sinful pleasures. This voice must proclaim, "There is another way!" There is the way of Jesus Christ, infinitely higher than the alluringly glamorous lotteries and spinning wheel rip-offs. This Christ is the only one who prevents the drain of creative vision and the hope of the beloved community from leaving the hearts and inner desires of all humanity. The modern world needs to hear anew the purity of the gospel of Jesus Christ, as Savior and

Lord of all life. He alone brings power that restores, refines, and relives life with great rejoicing.

Let the minister look beyond popularity to God who can give strength and guidance to all persons. God's power is available, and he freely shares it with the faithful. People, though they be sinners, still have some basic need to follow truth and respond to morality. There is no lasting satisfaction to those who bow to the popular gods of our times. Public acclamation of leadership and divine authorization of leadership are as far apart as night and day. The leaders of God must stand true to faith, even though countless masses go by to bow before worldly gods. In time they all will return, some to salvation, others to damnation, seeking the acclaim which only the universe will give.

## Expediency Versus a Blameless Ministry

Perfection in the Body of Christ is the only goal the minister can biblically justify. This goal was set before Abraham: ". . . walk before me, and be thou perfect" (Genesis 17:1). It was reaffirmed by our Lord in his Sermon on the Mount, "Be ye therefore perfect, even as your Father which is in heaven is perfect" (Matthew 5:48). Holiness, perfection, and blamelessness are spiritual synonyms that call the minister to the ultimate demands of the Christian faith. These demands are not impractical nor unrealistic. They say something about the process God takes persons through, making whole their lives. Holiness and blamelessness are not conditions achieved the moment one meets God. Such a jump would be unrealistic and would violate God's way of dealing with his people in Scripture.

The greatness of the Bible is found in its recurring realisms about life. Every condition, experience, or circumstance known to people is discussed in its pages. Men and women, such as Samson and Goliath, David and Paul, Rahab and Mary Magdalene, show us the depth to which we may fall but also the height we may attain. These living stories have not been left in Scripture to serve as fairy tales or entertaining literature. They are there to show that life requires hard struggle. God is sometimes seen permitting satanic forces to buffet persons. The Reverend Mark Riddix, of Baltimore, Maryland, stated: "God stretches man's life to create harmonic tension. Man, like a violin, must be stretched and attuned to do the full service of his Maker."[5]

The apostle Paul spoke at length on the warring struggles and tensions of life. As a gifted theologian, he keenly understood our earthly bodies and their longings for temporal pleasures. Paul spoke about the flesh as the seat of sin. "So then with the mind I myself serve the law of God; but with the flesh the law of sin" (Romans 7:25). This acknowledgment of humankind's lower nature did not keep Paul from reaching for the best. "For a bishop must be blameless, as the steward of God" (Titus 1:7). Paul knew that the process of becoming with God is fraught with perils and many temptations. We are never fully developed and faithful to God until God can trust us to deliver his word in all of life's tempting circumstances. Blamelessness as a spiritual goal is sterile without fully surrendering and living out the total abilities of one's days. Paul taught that this goal could be reached without worldly expediency and dangerous compromise.

The minister today is faced with a string of problems that almost defy solution. The questions of war and peace, abortion versus right to life, capital punishment and euthanasia—all are part of the baffling array of problems we face. Because of the press to find solutions to problems in our times, many ministers feel that expedience is the only way to come off without defeat. Such an attitude overlooks several things. It overlooks the fact that God's purpose in history, in our times, may necessitate the presence of these problems to humble and discipline an otherwise proud and arrogant people. It overlooks the fact that our solution to problems is not necessarily the solution God seeks. The Vietnam War is over, and a kind of solution has been reached. With displaced people, villages bombed, the need for food, jobs, medicine, and decent living, it is debatable whether the solution reached is the one God seeks. Surely there is a better way for people to live than the reported conditions which mark much of the life of present-day Vietnam. This attitude overlooks the fact that humankind's best answer to life's problems comes to us with built-in conditions that will plunge the human race into still further problems.

In such a world, the minister must not permit public complaints and misguided clamor to right all the world's wrongs keep one from seeing the basic moral predicament of the people. People today spotlight their ills on television, newspapers, and periodicals, while their basic illness is overlooked. People today have a need to know whether life has ultimate meaning. This need is keenly felt but seldom understood and articulated. Thus humanity runs to and fro seeking to occupy an otherwise wandering mind. All kinds of styles for clothes, spas for healthful living, diets for the good life, and meditation exercises for oneness with the universe have cropped up. The minister who fails to see the hectic activities of people today that often solve no problems will succumb to the same routine. It is hard to be an "Amos" and see through the conditions of today's lives and cry out what the real problem is! A broken relationship with God always produces a people who need endless substitutes for the true God. Crying out against this condition never takes the low road of expediency. Only the high road of a meaningful relationship with God will help people solve conditions that afflict today's lives with an ease of divine purpose and direction.

Expediency always exalts for a time the one bowing before its altar. It soothes problems but fails miserably to solve the sources of those problems. It seeks to deal with God mechanically, playing odds against various situations. Its chief weakness is its tendency to make its user selfish and without courage.

Urban America cannot be saved or permanently lifted with a leadership of expediency. Young men and women of urban ghettos already know a great deal about being slick. No doubt they have an advanced knowledge of rip-off artists, persons of insincerity, and the question of who really can be trusted. A cadre of inner-city ministers, working across color and denominational lines and upholding a blameless ministry, would be the beginning of a powerful leaven in the ghetto's moral morass.

No longer can many of the problems of teenage pregnancies, drug addiction, alcoholism, apparent loss of personal motivation, and general secular godlessness be lumped together as just symptomatic of the times. Dr. Martin Luther King, Jr., reminded us during his day that we needed to destroy the myths: (1) time is the only thing which can solve problems in civil rights. Time is neutral because it can be used either constructively or destructively. (2) Civil rights problems cannot be solved by legislation; hearts must be changed. However, while legislation can't change the heart, it can change persons' habits.[6] The church must use every avenue to make constructive use of time in the lives of people. The heavy loss of productive lives in urban America is a shame before the church, and a judgment of our weakness before God. No longer can the church and its ministry give up youth to worldly intoxications without at least openly waging aggressive wars for their souls. An all-out attack, by respected ministers of Christ, on the sources of moral corruption still makes a difference.

One of today's leaders in this field is the country preacher, the Reverend Jesse Jackson. In several interviews with him, he stated to me that he had a basic desire to see a renewal of traditional family, church, and community life that served well yesterday's generation. The Reverend Jackson is well aware that we live in a new age, but he believes the concept of the extended family still makes plenty of good sense. The harmonious working of home, church, and school provided character-molding discipline wherever these forces were at work.

> Jackson's feeling that permissive schools contribute to moral decay comes from his own memories of school in South Carolina. "I went to first grade in Greenville. Mrs. Georgia Robinson was the teacher. My mother knew her from the Springfield Baptist Church. So she took her and she said, 'Teach my boy all you can. Sometimes he gets unruly. If he does, use that strap on him.' And she said, 'I can't make most of the PTA meetings, but I'll see you at church on Sunday.' So between Mrs. Robinson, the church, and my mother I was in a love triangle. But it was also a discipline triangle."[7]

Jackson has also expressed serious concern over the illicit secular rhetoric that proliferates the airwaves of many of today's radio stations. Jackson sees a close connection between thinly disguised erotic language found in a lot of today's popular rock music, calling for people to "bump," "do it to me, Baby," "turn me on and let's go higher," and the moral decay destroying today's world. This type of mass entertainment, dispersed as a socially accepted way of life, ought to be attacked and exposed for what it is. Jackson's dream is not an illusion, but a necessary struggle if we are going to push back flowing tides of ungodliness. Pushing these tides back can be accomplished through a mighty coalition of Christian homes, schools, and churches. Today's generation must not be allowed to escape the discipline-love triangle Jackson referred to above.

A note of optimism was sounded for the church, especially the predominantly Black American church, by one of the Christian sages of our day. Dr. Carlyle Marney, executive director of Interpreter's House, Lake Junaluska, North Carolina, stated: "If I had to choose a church I have most hope for in America today, it would be the Black church. To date, it is not a slave of vested interests and is still free enough to do God's will."[8] The Black church must garner its moral, economic, spiritual, and numerical strength and become an even greater community for nurturing human souls. People of the inner city must be motivated to develop their finer selves. Sons and daughters must be motivated to go to colleges, pursue medical and judicial sciences, engineering, and ministering.

A heavier burden to do just this has been historically laid at the steps of the inner-city church. The crime, decay, and urban problems of today, though difficult to solve, nonetheless provide a great opportunity for the church to witness Jesus. Because walls of separation still divide large segments of peoples from sharing one with another, the inner-city church must not content itself simply to diagnose the problem. The Christian faith at heart is fundamentally healing in nature. It heals broken lives, restores shattered dreams, and stands masses up on their feet. The ministry of inner-city churches cannot hide behind walls but must aggressively seek people in house-to-house campaigns, radio and television ministries. It is in such ministering that God out of his amazing powers turns broken lives into soldiers of the cross.

The highly successful book entitled *Roots,* by Alex Haley, has proved the validity of knowing as much as possible about one's background. In a conversation I asked Alex Haley what the great inspiration urging him to pursue his work was. He answered, "A grandmother who had left in me a deep faith in God, in the history of my people. She used to say, 'God may not come when you want him, but he is always on time!'" I wonder how many persons who have read Mr. Haley's work have observed the deep piety that continued to surface in prayer language, faith in God, baptism, and rugged hope that passed on from generation to generation.

The ministry of power today can learn from this tradition. All of us can use the creative flow of past traditions better to serve this present age. We can all draw from past puritan tradition in American life, rich in work ethic, grounded in piety and in respect of church and state. We can draw from the tradition of slaves, who left us an oral tradition in theology, prayer language, and song style. Any ethnic tradition that serves the present age and calls persons to a deeper knowledge of God should be used and passed on to unborn generations.

Many persons in today's culture will not be reached by a cold, highly intellectual theology that does not readily speak to human needs. Scholarship of any description is futile if it fails to communicate and lead people to a fuller understanding of their lives with God. The Black ministry today must especially be alert to the needs of Black people, in the light of who they are and from whence they have come. They have a peculiar, oppressive history!

This is no call for a ministry devoid of excellence. Excellence in the Christian church prefers the best in music, literature, worship order, and style. A sad commentary on today's church is its failure to use the great slave songs. "Swing Low, Sweet Chariot," "Steal Away to Jesus," and "Lord, I Want to Be a Christian" are examples of ageless messages in song that point all lives to God. Songs of faith and hymns of inspiration ought to undergird theology, support Christian creeds, and build up the Body of Christ. Nothing can be left to chance in a creative, blameless ministry.

Mr. Hiram Lane, deacon of New Shiloh Baptist Church, Baltimore, Maryland, made this comment to me: "Reverend, people today are just too weak-minded! Too weak-minded! All that cheap religious music on radio. No Bible, don't mean a thing! I like Shiloh because I hear here the old hymns and spirituals we sang in Texas. I like those hymns, 'A Charge to Keep I Have,' 'Jacob's Ladder,' 'Father, I Stretch My Hand to Thee.' These hymns have a message and they give me power." Hiram Lane rejected the soothing lullabies of lines and rhythm so closely attuned to worldly sounds as to be almost indistinguishable.

I asked a ministers' seminar class, composed of Baptist pastors of the city of Baltimore, Maryland, the following question: "What are the major hindrances to a sound, effective ministry in our times?" I wanted to compare their thinking with the response given by Hiram Lane. The following answers were given: (1) The inability to take the Bible and make it relevant in an age of moral decay. (2) Failure to find the necessary motivation and time for creative work. (3) The secular mind set of today's generation that seems to bog down effective preaching. (4) Finding the inspiration to pursue excellence in one's work.

All of the answers reflect heavily on the heavy negative influence today's world exerts on the minister. They call to our attention the loss of power and faith that is inevitable when one loses the root of one's faith and majors on the passing styles and shadows. A blameless ministry is not achieved in the world; it is achieved in the Body of Christ. The sense of living for Jesus Christ can override the moral quagmire of today. Our institutions may be corrupt, but the prophetic ministry of "Thus saith the Lord" has broken down demonic empires before and surely will do it again. As the minister works through the biblical texts of old, they will become new in her or his own life, for her or his own people, in the here and now. New soldiers of Israel will march out of their present Egyptian slaveries and praise God forever in Canaan lands. People of God will again relive exodus experiences, sustained by mighty covenants that cause people to know we are the elect of God. A new dynamism will be released bursting forth tides of divine inspiration, and walls of Jericho will still come tumbling down. The call to minister will always demand the very best from God's servant. It is the ultimate of human pursuits, involving a marriage between God and a person.

In this chapter, we have seen how concupiscence can grip the minister with a robe of ease, well-being, carefree living, and fleeting freedom. We have seen the theological wardrobe of this myth. It is sanctified with a false holiness as it is handed down from one generation to another. It crops up during moments of conventions and associational meetings and robs the work of God from a unified attack against the armies of the evil one. It seeks to do through popularity and expediency what it fails to do through sincere service to Christ. Because it overlooks the full power of the Word of God, the church suffers, and masses languish for a liberating word from God. All of this happens when biblical knowledge is lacking and joys of the flesh are freely enjoyed. Rising above this myth can indeed be done. The finest text of Jesus' greatness is found in these words, "For we have not an high priest which cannot be touched with the feeling of our infirmities; but was in all points tempted like as we are, yet without sin" (Hebrews 4:15).

In the next chapter we will look at the church control myth. Is the minister the absolute boss of the local congregation? Is there any meaningful distinction between controlling the flock and shepherding the flock? Is there not serious danger in prestige fights, standing pastor against others, power blocs, and cliques in the church? Let us examine this difficult myth and try to find God's way to a richer ministry.

# The Church Control Myth

# 5

The first major problem Adam and Eve had in the Garden of Eden involved power and control. "And the LORD God commanded the man, saying, Of every tree of the garden thou mayest freely eat: But of the tree of the knowledge of good and evil, thou shalt not eat of it: for in the day that thou eatest thereof thou shalt surely die" (Genesis 2:16-17). The moral subtlety of this problem is universal in type and character. People never seem to content themselves with what they have, but constantly search for more. God reserved only one tree for himself; yet it was that one tree that tested the moral strength of Adam and Eve. The problem of power is always a moral one. What power does to the one who has it and how one uses power in human relationships are the major moral tests of life.

Every beginning minister is tempted to want to taste of all the trees in the garden, just as did Adam and Eve. One wants to survey the grounds, drive in the stakes, and post the "No Trespassing" signs. The sovereign nature of the minister cries out to be known, respected, and confirmed by the congregation. Paradoxically, one's desire for power and influence with the congregation is often strongest when there has been no reason to justify the same. Adam and Eve never did enjoy the glory of walking with God, growing in his love, and coming to have power with him. They wanted influence and power before they lived to know and love the garden. Many ministers have been told they are the bosses of their congregations. All too often they proceed to take control before they have surveyed the land.

Conflicts over pastoral control develop in many ways. The first will be discussed under the heading of confrontation. Confrontation occurs when two opposing powers meet with no clear knowledge of the outcome. There is always the possibility of confrontation in which the will of one party seeks to carry through a program diametrically opposed by another. These moments of opposition bear the need of serious study since they tend to divide people into opposing factions that often obscure the true mission of the church.

## Confrontation

Court Street Baptist Church prided itself on having a strong official board where seniority was observed with reverence, permitting senior officers to exert tremendous influence. Over the years the board had won the allegiance of the church in such a way that it was permitted literally to run the affairs of the congregation. The chairman of the deacon board had secured his position through a kind of political savvy and the support of key persons in the congregation. The vice-chairman of the board was a man of wide influence who had a phenomenal ability to remember names and addresses of many families. His major work as an insurance manager had made him quite a strong community personality. Together these two men had great influence on the church, literally controlled the board, and thought their minister should preach the Word and tend to the flock and leave the job of running the church to the officers.

I was called to this church at twenty-two years of age, straight out of seminary. Since this was my first full-time church, the nature and traditions of this well-established historic church could offer problems if not handled wisely. For example, the board of the church met in the insurance office of the vice-chairman. The meeting had an air of levity and civic fraternity, devoid of sacred and sincere purpose. Cigarettes were smoked and jokes were exchanged. I knew then that it was practically impossible to do work for the Master so far removed from the sanctity of Zion. The pastor did not preside but sat as an obligated member of the group.

The same carefree attitude of the board meetings was felt in the service of worship. The officers sat on the extreme right side of the very large church, almost out of view of the pulpit. I knew that the church, founded in the year 1833, had succumbed to a worship of tradition, sacred history, and it needed spiritual renewal. I knew that only the gospel of Jesus Christ could bring about the renaissance of fellowship available to all in the Body of Christ.

One Sunday morning following a moving worship experience, I stated before the benediction: "The pastor would like to speak with all officers of the church in the lower auditorium immediately following the benediction." In this meeting I expected to have the spiritual initiative for several reasons. I was the pastor! The Lord had blessed us with a glorious worship! Calling the meeting at this time provided me a necessary spiritual initiative to say what was upon my heart. I informed the officers that I would no longer meet with them to do church business outside the sacred walls of church and declared my total purpose to strengthen the Christian life of the church. I marshaled the officers to help in winning Lynchburg, Virginia, to Christ! The spiritual strategy paid off! The business meeting place was changed to the church. The seating of officers was moved to the center of the congregation, and the real beginning of a spiritual renewal was launched!

This confrontation would have been unwise if made during a regular meeting of the board. In church life, many ministers run into serious opposition because the visions they see are not necessarily seen by the people. At least in the Protestant church, one of the main sources of lasting power is the pulpit. Great preaching prepares the way for the growth of God's people. Great biblical preaching can turn confrontations into redeeming experiences where all the people of God will be blessed.

In the same congregation, I once overlooked a funeral engagement. In the rush of pastoral appointments, I inadvertently forgot a late afternoon funeral parlor service of a member. The following Sunday morning the board called me in for a conference. "Reverend," said the chairman, "why is it you failed to attend Sister Mitchell's funeral this past Thursday at 4 P.M.? What happened?" The possibility for an explosive event was in the air. There was a sense of the preacher being on trial. Furthermore, I knew this event could have serious influence on pastoral days to come. I quickly remembered what the old sage, J. Pius Barbour, had said in a conversation I had with him in his home: "Whenever you find yourself in a jam with your officers, and no major principles are at stake, take low! Ain't no harm to take low! After all, you are the pastor and the folks are looking at you!"

I answered in this way, "Brethren, I have no excuse. In the business of doing the Lord's work, a lot of things come up, and this one slipped by me." Immediately one of the deacons, seldom heard, spoke up and said, "Brethren, let our pastor alone. We all have overlooked some things in our life." The meeting broke up with the shaking of hands and the rise of a deeper sense of the humanity and divinity in us all.

Dealing with people is a guarantee that confrontation of some type will eventually happen. When it is continued as a means of controlling persons, counterforces of unpredictable power can result. Samuel McKinney related how he avoided a damaging confrontation and built a one and one-half million dollar church: "It took me many years. I knew when I was going into a board meeting and overheard one of the sisters saying, 'Come on, let's go on in here and build Rev. McKinney's church.' I knew then I had to freeze this project until a later day." A later day came sooner than McKinney expected. "Nature cooperated with me in the old church building. One Sunday morning during a heavy rainstorm, the roof leaked very heavily over the senior choir, soiling the Sunday finery of the saints. I saw the heavy drops and silently said, 'Thank you, Jesus!'" Not many Sundays later another gust of rain descended on the roof of the building, this time hitting the deacons and bursting through the deteriorated stained-glass windows. Again the pastor said in silence, "Thank you, Jesus!" Gradually the Reverend McKinney's church became "Our Church!"

The wise minister will use the virtue of patience and seize those moments when truth and goodwill break through, in spite of disturbing circumstances. Something is lost when the minister has to side with one of several opposing forces in the church over various issues in such a way as to damage the effectiveness of one's ministry. Given time, patience, and serious prayer, a moment will come in every disturbing situation where the minister can decide for the good of everyone. This does not call for a passive, timid, or indecisive ministry. It does call for weighing the options and acting for the good of the people. People see Christ in places other than the pulpit. Some see Christ in the way leaders deal with those one serves, especially in trying circumstances. Evil forces have historically sought to anger those in authority, tempting them to see if they would forsake their God.

The wise minister will know when to stand firm regardless of circumstances or personalities involved. The Spirit of God ministers to those who trust him and seek the guidance of his light. This is why the prophets of old were known as Spirit filled! This is why John the Baptizer was able to stand up against his hearers who came out to test and try his ministry! This is why Jesus made the Spirit of God an absolute requisite for those persons going out to minister in his name. "But when they deliver you up, take no thought how or what ye shall speak: for it shall be given you in that same hour what ye shall speak" (Matthew 10:19).

The minister's whole personality says a lot about where one is going. The Gospel narrative reveals how the personality and the mission became one in the life of Jesus Christ. His mere presence was an occasion for confrontation.

> And it came to pass, when the time was come that he should be received up, he stedfastly set his face to go to Jerusalem. And sent messengers before his face: and they went, and entered into a village of the Samaritans, to make ready for him. And they did not receive him, because his face was as though he would go to Jerusalem (Luke 9:51-53).

The mission of God in the life of Jesus Christ was stronger than temporal, political, or materialistic concerns. Those who saw him saw total dedication to the purpose of God! In spite of death itself, Jesus went to the cross because of the power of love. Divine confrontation with the forces of hell was the only way resurrection reality would eternalize all the claims of our Lord. This ultimate confrontation that produced eternal life is a living testimony to every minister that the law of love finally demands one's all!

In the inevitable struggle for power, confrontation does not stand alone. Exploitation is another pitfall that often mires a promising ministry. Unlike officer-controlled churches where confrontations are always threatening possibilities, exploitation seems to be a temptation where congregations express deep faith in their minister and give one a free rein in the control and pastoring of the church.

## Exploitation

New Shiloh Baptist Church is a fellowship founded in the year 1901 which has had across those years three pastors. The congregation has a rich tradition of respecting the pastor and according him an abundance of trust. The church generally accepts the teaching that Christ is the head of his church and the pastor ought to be afforded honor and respect as an undershepherd of Jesus Christ. The reader can imagine what a change I felt coming from a church where every decision had to be debated and discussed to be approved to a church where members expected the pastor to make decisions and provide leadership. "Reverend, can our auxiliary have this date for this particular service?" "How much money can we give to this or that cause?" "What is your opinion on this matter, from personal concerns to ecclesiastical considerations?"

In this atmosphere of trust, exploitation of the people's goodwill is an ever-present temptation. Generally people are exploited for quick materialistic gains. Ministers are not usually persons of worldly wealth, and some exploit their following for their own gain. In this kind of shady ministerial dealings, one is liable to justify one's selfish proclivities by declaring them part and parcel of the calling. The turning of light to darkness in the work of the ministry is not easily noticed by the sinful eye. Therefore the problem of exploitation cannot be brushed aside as unimportant. The "least ones" with God determine the well-being of the minister's course. (See Matthew 25:45.)

When the sense of duty is not strong, and the call to service is faintly felt, the possibility of exploiting a trusting people for self-serving ends increases in zeal. The minister overcomes this problem by seeking power through service to others. Love must be expressed in ways and actions beyond the pulpit! My own background with Dr. Martin Luther King, Jr., has convinced me that a total gospel provides far more to people than it begs in return. When it fails to give succor for living, and strength for every day, its reason for existence is in doubt. People trust leaders because they want liberation. Many see their lives caught in the industrial machinery of our day and wonder if it is all worthwhile. Still others have been forced from one community to another, seeking jobs and the promise of a bright future for their children. They come to church as the only place they can give allegiance to a leadership that matters and makes a difference! Sham leaders who take advantage of that trust and translate it into short-lived gains are an abomination in the sight of God.

The freedom inherent in the Christian ministry is awesome. Persons unable to order their lives or divert their steps will fake many excuses for service. Theologians have told us that the freedom God gave to us in creation left in us the possibility of rebellion against God. The book of Acts records the trust the early church gave to the apostolic leadership. ". . . as many as were possessors of lands or houses sold them, and brought the prices of the things that were sold, And laid them down at the apostles' feet: and distribution was made unto every man according as he had need" (Acts 4:34-35). The only overseer the apostles had was God. The story reveals God's approval for people trusting their ministers but also points to the need for ministers to prove worthy of that trust.

Another aspect of exploitation is its tendency toward self-edification. When moral foundations are broken, substitute gods enthrone themselves. This is true with the Christian ministry that thrives on being seen and heard as the final word, the final voice. Homage must be paid to the ministry as that which holds the program and the people together. No dissent whatsoever is tolerated. One never knows what dissent will uncover when moral foundations are shaky. A rigid and stern loyalty to the minister is a religious duty. It is that prime duty that assures one a seat in the kingdom. Now that the minister is a self-made god, one relinquishes any rights to publicly exposed human frailties. One now projects an image of human indestructibility.

Jesus pronounced strong words against exploiters of the flock. "It is impossible but that offences will come: but woe unto him, through whom they come! It were better for him that a millstone were hanged about his neck, and he cast into the sea, than that he should offend one of these little ones" (Luke 17:1-2). Jesus would not endorse a ministry that used people for personal glory. Jesus in effect was evolving a radical shift in his teachings on ministry. No longer were people to be ripped off in houses of worship, under the cloud of the holy! No longer were people expected to pay homage and reverence to holy leaders without being ministered to by those leaders. Jesus taught from the beginning that continued blessing lines can never substitute for a sacred altar of total self-surrender, nor could worldly gain substitute for the fundamental service the Christian minister owes to the people of God.

Martin Luther King, Jr., had an unusual ability to hold those ministerial tensions in balance. He enjoyed life fully but never permitted comforts or material gains to keep him from a life of sacrifice for the good of others. His temptations to live a life of ease were augmented by a middle-class church, with a highly educated and professional congregation, and a family background that provided him with many comforts of earthly life. I learned how to put all these things in balance, working with this man. Behind the veneer of titles, professions, social and ethnic classes, all persons stand naked before God and desperately need to know God's Word. All persons need to be challenged to share in building the common bond of humanity with a full understanding of the fatherhood of God and the brotherhood and sisterhood of persons. The year I spent with this man of God convinced me that one can enjoy clothes, food, shelter, transportation, arts, material goods, so long as they do not come between one's soul and the Savior.

Many of Dr. King's critics have made much ado about his eating, travel, and dressing habits. They remind us that he lived in suites, was chauffer driven and police escorted through cities, and was a kind of regal king. What these cynics overlook is that the limousines and suites never kept Dr. King from meeting duty whenever found, or going to jail, boldly risking his life for the cause of truth. His last destined trip to Memphis forever sealed the fact that his life was committed to service.

Association with Dr. King gave me a healthy attitude about the nature of God and his love of the world. God intended for persons to celebrate life. For that cause God gave his Son, Jesus Christ, to show us in earthbound ways how to live in perfect harmony a life of celebration with God. Exploitation of this world or the people of the world is an act of defiance against God's ordered purposes. Christianity cannot blossom under self-serving causes, but it blossoms through the lives of dedicated persons, who celebrate life in harmony with God's will. Dr. King was definitely celebrating life's finest virtues when he identified in the struggle to help sanitation workers, domestics, and the forgotten people of society. Celebration is really the song of human liberation. It is sung by those who know · by actions that Christianity is heaven's battalion of disciples waging war on the ungodliness and inhumanity of humankind. Only this call to duty and commitment will make a difference in the service of Christ. This is a terrible need for our day when life's celebration has been shifted from the struggle of the human soul to the fleeting sounds of humankind that fail to lift the spirit or make the wounded whole.

James Peters, former executive minister of American Baptist Churches of the South, stated:

> Churches that are making a difference throughout the sixteen states region of the south are those churches with pastors who have supported community causes across the years. These men were supporters of the civil rights movement. They supported Black colleges, seminaries, and other Christian institutions. They are the principle supporters of Fund of Renewal today.[1]

Dr. Peters has witnessed from his vantage point a striking and significant difference between those persons with a love for causes and those without. He stated that they can be counted upon not simply to support one cause, but to help humanity beyond normal limitations.

The minister leaving seminary today ought to be prepared to serve and support Christian causes. The high cost of higher education is already beyond the reach of the average student. Many youth, already afflicted with a weakened motivation for educational growth, will easily fall by the way without a strong church. The highest loss to any great nation is that of minds that failed to blossom. With all of America's technological advances, the best route to the mainstream of this culture, especially for minority students, is through higher education. When families see in the minister a strong model for educational excellence, they will have a much greater motivation to educate themselves and to make the necessary sacrifices for their children.

The need for continued support of traditional Black colleges and seminaries is critical. These schools have served a historic role, developing men and women when other educational doors were closed. They have not only served as a remedial gap for many minorities deprived of strong high school backgrounds, but also have gone on to mold many giants from this pool of humanity. These schools deserve unlimited support from the Christian church. They were born to meet the needs of a disfranchised people and now enjoy a long heritage of surviving on meager fares. Where would minority leadership be today if there had been no colleges or seminaries geared to their level of need, molding lives into finished products? I contend that minority leadership in ministry must do much more than it is now doing to keep minority institutions alive. There comes a time when those who have been deprived rise up and minister to those who did the depriving. The day has come for the American Black Church, especially, to rise above primary concerns for self and local surroundings and reach out collectively, building greater structures upon the institutional foundations already bequeathed to us by our elders.

More persons are reached when the Christian church rallies around institutional causes. Persons who might not attend the church still come under the influence of Christ in a denominationally sponsored school. Teachers with a consciousness of Christ can help many lives faced with crossroad experiences between God and the world. Isolated ministers, tempted to build self-made kingdoms, will be made to appear exactly who they are. When Christ is in the center of a great ministry, the total care of his people will be a priority, and the spiritual development of people will follow.

### Negotiations

Negotiation is the practice of sitting down with persons of opposing views and powers, seeking a ground of understanding, and working through to a common agreement. The minister called to pastor a local church usually will have some initial conference where one is expected to sit down and discuss all matters relating to one's pastoral relationship with the church. Those items could include the pastor's salary, housing, transportation, denominational-related travel, vacation, retirement, and the authority of the pulpit. By simple principles of business, some of these matters have to be discussed and agreed upon. Some have to do with the minister's peculiar authority as a preacher who pastors God's people. A sense of direction and a knowledge of the vital difference in these matters are absolutely necessary in a meaningful ministry.

This initial conference is usually held without too much conflict, given the people's interest in their newly called pastor. Lack of conflict should not be interpreted as a basic sign of goodwill. Goodwill is born out of understanding and mutual trust. It comes out of the process of learning to know, love, and fully accept the strengths and to deal with the weaknesses of one another. This is why conflicts and various problems in Christian ministry tend to rise after the pastor's beginning honeymoon relationship with the flock wears thin, and the minister's personality, like that of the flock's, begins to emerge. Both leader and people have been scrutinizing the other to learn all possible. The people have certainly looked on the pastor to determine: "What kind of shepherd do we have? To whom does the pastor relate? What is the substance and style of the pastor's sermons? Is the minister really sincere? Who controls the pastor, and how does the pastor relate to other ministers and churches?" These concerns can go on and on with no coherent order. In the present age of television consciousness, they also include personal styles, images, and general personal demeanor.

There is no period in the minister's public life when one is not eliciting some kind of reaction from others. Being aware of this fact does not place an undue burden upon the minister, but does cause one to be aware of the total impact of one's life. Friends made today could easily be tomorrow's enemies. The minister may have said something or acted in a certain way that alienated someone without any awareness of the fact at all. This is why it is so important for the minister to lift up a standard for the people to see beyond self. When they see "Self," agonies and problems will be many. When they see "The Word of God ministering through self," they have to mortify petty concerns while seeking to fulfill the demands of God's Word.

Among Jesus' last major instructions to his disciple were the following words: "Simon, son of Jonas, lovest thou me more than these? . . . He saith unto him, Feed my lambs. He saith to him again the second time, Simon, son of Jonas, lovest thou me? He saith unto him, Yea, Lord; thou knowest that I love thee. He saith unto him, Feed my sheep" (John 21:15-16). Peter, all the flock, young and old,

are important to me. You must minister to them with divine
substance that matters. Many situations will seek to claim your
attention and divert you from building up lives. Many issues will
seem important, and you will be tempted to relegate gospel truths.
You must feed the sheep without regard to differences of the kind or
quality of sheep!

Jesus calls the minister to see the difference between feeding the
sheep and negotiating with the sheep. Feeding the sheep keeps the
minister in the heart of one's calling. To be an ambassador demands
knowing what one's message is. It requires the utmost skill in winning
friends as a representative of the government one serves. Feeding the
sheep enlarges the mind and challenges the holistic growth of both
shepherd and flock. When feeding is not properly done, negotiations
pop up to determine the course on which the church will move. Quite
often the need to negotiate grows out of alliances with cliques and
buddies in the church. All of this runs counter to Jesus' call to feed.
Cliques and buddies, whoever they are, have no kingdom to give and
cannot be expected to deliver saving power in the crucial day of
testing. Jesus eliminated the buddy system through his forthright
example to Legion whom he had now made whole: "Go home to thy
friends, and tell them what great things the Lord hath done for thee,
and hath had compassion on thee" (Mark 5:19). Jesus turned the
man's felt indebtedness to him into a positive outreaching flow of
community service. No ministers who make disciples in the name of
the Lord will ever see their powers negotiated away or limited.

Wise pastors will use their power to recruit and make soldiers who
will go back home and help redeem broken communities. The
movement of Christian ministry is always directed toward redeeming
others. Real love grows outward in proportion as it grows inward.
The tragedy of having to negotiate to sustain one's ministry is the fact
that it is not built upon growth, nor building up the Body of Christ. It
has to lobby on issues that quite often are not eternal, substituting
human conditions that need transforming for the edifying presence of
Christ. When the negotiation sessions are over, who is left on fire for
Christ? The secret of feeding the flock is to empower others so they
will be able to empower still others with the saving word of God.

Negotiation sessions brought on by confrontations ought to be
avoided if possible. The minister has received a certain authority

given by God. That authority, sharpened through prayer, devotional life, and theological training, presupposes a certain ability to know where one is going and to give clear orders to the flock. When that authority is questioned and compromised through weak ministerial leadership, the whole church suffers. People need to hear a clear, concise, and forceful word from the Lord. They need to know God's servant is being led by a Higher Power, as they stake their lives on the pastor's claims!

The minister must know that his or her pulpit is therefore non-negotiable. The word spoken from the pulpit should be the authentic, inspired Word of God. It must not be dictated by the selfish whims of interest groups and self-serving persons. Who goes into the pulpit and what one does after arriving are sacred rights only the minister ought to exercise. The minister's personal and private life should be lived in such way that it is nonnegotiable. A minister's circle of friends should include everyone one meets. This type of behavior will enhance harmony in the fellowship and help to anchor everyone in the true Christian faith.

Christian congregations have a right to expect sainted strength, profound hope, and deep faith in the shepherd. Whatever the theological positions of the laity regarding the clergy, nothing rules out people's instinctive need to see determined leadership in the one up front. They want to believe God's leader is marching with determination toward Jerusalem, willing to face whatever Armageddon that might await one's life. They want to hear the leader cry out against sin, against entrenched social evils wherever found, while serving as a moral conscience to one's generation, lifting up a holy ideal. Every Christian sooner or later learns that the heart of the Christian faith is a cross that our Lord refused to negotiate, but accepted with triumphant resolve. "Not my will, Lord, but thy will be done!" (See Matthew 26:42.)

The minister's freedom is to obey God. That freedom was secured through our Lord's triumph over death and resurrection from the dead. The minister is now free to be a slave of Jesus Christ and not a puppet of the world. Here is a freedom to support the cause of truth, to identify and liberate the world's captive people, and to show the way to salvation to persons lost in life's dark maze. Here is a freedom that makes God's servant an ambassador of truth with full powers to act with love upon the lives of others. This freedom resists the erosion of worldly temptations to share sacred powers! It refuses to sell its soul for a mess of pottage. It remembers the words of Jesus Christ who said, "No man, having put his hand to the plough, and looking back, is fit for the kingdom of God" (Luke 9:62).

Having discussed all this, what option is left for the minister to deal with the flock? How does one go about getting one's programs through, dealing with matters of state, and smoothly running the ecclesiastical machinery? Confrontations often injure others. Negotiations run the risk of compromising sacred principles and eroding the power of forthright leadership. There must be a better way, and there is! It is the way of exaltation.

## Exaltation

"And I, if I be lifted up from the earth, will draw all men unto me" (John 12:32). The beginning and ending of the Christian faith are wrapped up in the person of Jesus Christ. Ministers must know all they can about Jesus, and the spirit of Jesus must be intimately alive in ministers' lives. The road of learning and knowing more and more about Jesus is a full lifetime's pilgrimage! Any minister who day by day finds some meaningful way to lift up the saving name of Jesus Christ will not wander adrift in life's sea. Failure to restudy the life and message of Jesus Christ is analogous to children who leave home and never write, return a call, or check simply to see how their parents are getting along. The children assume that the parents who raised them are well able to go on living independently. They overlook the desire of the parents to share continually the growth patterns, the high experiences, even the sorrows that may come into children's lives. God's love to humankind has been given in Jesus Christ. Christ through his church desires to share with persons, day by day, in a common growing experience of love. It is this growing experience of love that provides the power to lift Jesus up. When the messianic personality of Jesus Christ is lost in the lives of believers, what is left are the bare teachings of mortals. Exaltation of Christ means going beyond human personality to accept by faith what the Bible testified about Jesus Christ. In birth he was exalted as the Son of God, born of the virgin Mary, in the fullness of time. (See Matthew 1:21-23.) Along the course of his ministry he was continually exalted by God far above others, in that his oneness with the Godhead was proclaimed. During his baptism, the heavens opened and a voice resounded saying, "Thou art my beloved Son, in whom I am well pleased" (Mark 1:11). Jesus declared that the mighty works he did were meant to exalt faith and glorify God. (See John 9:3-5.) His transfiguration experience was another event when God broke through and declared Jesus as the One worthy to be heard.

The theologian Wolfhart Pannenberg, in his book *Jesus—God and Man,* talks about the finality of the life, work, death, and resurrection of Jesus. One of his basic emphases is that God has forever vindicated the life and work of Jesus through the event of the resurrection. Therefore, Jesus Christ is worthy of worship and praise.

> If the resurrection or the appearances of the resurrected Jesus were only brute facts without inherent significance, then, certainly, the origin of faith would not be understandable from this event. . . . Jesus' resurrection and the Christian hope of resurrection involve a life completely different from all life with which we are familiar, an imperishable life no longer limited by death, which at any rate, therefore, must be basically different from the organic form of life with which we are familiar.[2]

When we affirm Christ, we are saying to the world that God has acted in Jesus Christ in such a way that human salvation through him is now possible, and the end of all the ages has divine purpose and direction.

Exalting Jesus Christ is the secret of the church's ability to renew itself, to trust anew with boundless evidences of infinite power. Such evidences are widely proclaimed at the present time. Some theologians are telling us that men and women are seeking to find new meaning in the person of Jesus Christ. Large numbers are claiming to have had born-again experiences and to have been filled with the presence of the Holy Ghost. This renewal of interest in Jesus is showing among Jewish scholars. A *New York Times* article entitled "Jewish Scholars Reassessing Historical Jesus" stated that many in the Jewish community have "an eagerness and curiosity to know" more about this subject. They are discovering that when Jesus is studied from the Jewish perspective, Jesus was a good Jew with a strong sense of religious mission.[3] How this new interest will affect an embracing of Jesus as Lord among Jews remains to be seen. At least some youthful Jews have already made that confession.

In an article in *Time* magazine entitled "Yeshua Is the Messiah," it was stated that "since the late 1960s, perhaps 10,000 to 20,000 young U.S. Jews have decided to follow Jesus." Asked why young American Jews are turning to Jesus, "Donald LeMagdeleine, a Roman Catholic who is conducting the first careful survey of the young converts for a thesis at Berkeley's Graduate Theological Union, [states]: 'They want a religious experience that they did not find in their synagogues or in Jewish cultural upbringing. . . . They are not looking for Jewish rap groups. They are looking for God.'"[4]

What does this movement of interest in Jesus among Jews and what do the mass born-again experiences say to us about exaltation of Jesus Christ? They reveal a divine initiative at work in the lifting up of Jesus' life. It is an initiative that defies the erosion of history which usually pulls the curtain down on other great lives. It reveals that the minister whose life is committed to exalting Christ works with the force of God on one's side. With such a renewal of emphasis on the life of Jesus, the Christian minister ought to strive all the more to be intellectually sound and morally upright in one's ministry of the Son of God. In a world of spreading religious sects, oriental faiths and cults, satanic and mystery religions, a new and revitalized relationship with Christ will do wonders for all believers in our times. Christ alone can still liberate bound and broken humanity from laws of legalism, empty liturgies, and meaningless sacred practices devoid of saving substance. He alone saves and liberates and makes each life whole and complete!

In a meeting of the Baptist World Alliance, Chester J. Jump, Jr., Executive Director of International Ministries of the American Baptist Churches, reported in a commission on communications that the most effective means of communicating the gospel message is the local pastor, and second to the local pastor is information carried on his or her bulletins. This was good news in a world supposedly dominated by television news coverage and newsprint of all descriptions. The local pastor still has power to lift up Jesus and command genuine attention. The minister's message can still break the secular news monopoly and proclaim Christ as Savior and Lord of life.

The Christian minister should never underestimate his or her awesome power to communicate. The same Christ of Bethlehem can be communicated to persons in ghetto flats and space-age colonies. All language can be used to communicate his word, from the scholastic semantics of scholars to the vernacular jargon of everyday life. The only concern that matters is to communicate him. Something happens in the communications. Babies are blessed, and the hungry find jobs. Houses are built and neighborhoods become communities of love. The sick are healed and the weak are made strong. Bent backs are straightened and persons live and move in God. In the proclamation of the word, the miracle of human transformation occurs. Earthbound lives are transformed by the renewing power of the Word. What a challenge and blessed hope the minister today has to lift the name of Jesus! Beyond the pulpit and the bulletins, one has television, radio, communication satellites, and sound systems. Rather than worrying about controlling the local church, ministers must let their hearts melt, just as Jesus did, when they look on the masses moving about as sheep without a shepherd. (See Matthew 9:36.) The vision of Christ always points toward humanity, wherever found. There the sincere minister of Jesus Christ feeds God's people with the sacred Bread of Life.

Growing into the fullness of the stature of Jesus Christ is a biblical requisite for all ages and groups. Myths are not confined to adults; they creep with deathly powers upon the lives of youth, robbing many of productive Christ-filled lives. Adults are often used to reinforce questionable youthful trends. In my own ministry, one of the questions I have heard many times is, "How do you hold your young people in the church?" I have answered that I hold none of them; the power of Christ holds them! Of course many reasons have prompted people to ask this question. Young people, especially in late teenage days, have been victimized by loss of church commitment. Surely there must be some reasons. The next chapter will discuss this matter under the theme "The Childhood and Youth Myth."

# The Childhood and Youth Myth

# 6

The present age in American culture has been popularly called "The Age of the Youth." When John Fitzgerald Kennedy, thirty-fifth president of the United States of America, announced in his inaugural message that his generation must conquer "The New Frontiers" of American life, a new spirit of optimism was released to combat life's ageless problems of hunger, poverty, war, and disease, and cause citizens to seek peace, love, and mutual fidelity. Already the civil rights movement under the leadership of Martin Luther King, Jr., had emphasized the community of all persons and their basic rights as written out and declared by the Constitution of the United States and the basic word of God. America, land of the brave and home of the free, was called upon to honor her commitments to all of her sons and daughters, in her public marketplaces, her myriad places of employment, and at the bar of justice. Everywhere there was the sense that the nation was on the march, and students were largely in the forefront of that march. Youth left classrooms, comfortable homes, and went to Mississippi, Alabama, Georgia, and other places of civic interest, to declare themselves for open public accommodations and equal opportunities for all. Many were locked in jails, thereby arousing public consciousness against unjust laws of society that had been used to subdue minorities. A new sense of sexual liberation stripped puritanical codes of the past away, and lobbied for liberty in sexual affairs. Pornographic magazines proliferated newsstands, proclaiming the adventures locked in the human body and the erotic thrills of free sex. The age of Aquarius had arrived. In matters religious, youth often commanded center stage by rejecting the established church as an institution of frozen and inflexible experience and declaring their parents had lost their way. They took to the woods establishing social communes, sharing both parental and food responsibilities, while becoming adherents of newly discovered religions and oriental cults. Many discovered Jesus and became known as Children of God, as well as Jesus Freaks.

Today the tenor of much of the radical aspects of the youth movements born out of the 1960s has dissipated due to many things. The questionable involvement of our nation in the Vietnam War has had a sobering effect on everyone. The whole economic picture of the nation, with the overriding need for jobs and personal security, has helped to build a conservative American spirit. Revelations uncovered by the Watergate era of American political life also shifted attention from causes previously espoused by youth. Notwithstanding these and other developments, the church has come through them all, with a lingering notion that children and youth ought to be won and held by the minister. While the world has marched forward with all kinds of invitations to command our children and youth, all too often the church has relegated the important task of recruiting and challenging this age group to the minister, who is only one of the important pillars of society.

Congregations want to know how ministers relate with young persons. They want to know whether the minister is able to win their sons and daughters back to church. They are quick to say, "We need a minister who will create a program that will interest our youth and keep them out of trouble!" These are all good intentions. They assume even greater weight when it is realized that alcohol is one of the major problems causing youth today to be involved in so much crime and so many traffic accidents. In a study at Johns Hopkins University Research Center, 1978, it was reported that youth in ever-increasing numbers today are drinking. The implications are enormous. Drug involvement, crime, broken homes, and social sickness are all spin-offs of the disease of alcoholism. Yet no minister can adequately deal with and solve these congregational desires for their youth without total church support!

Built into these good desires and intentions are hidden Trojan horses. There are serious reservations whether a minister can be free to minister to everyone who has been saddled with the demands of winning the youth. People often throw on leaders responsibilities for their own shortcomings and failures. The minister is not a scapegoat for prodigal sons and wayward daughters. An obsessive emphasis on youth has the probability of creating a church for youth versus a church for adults. Everyone in the congregation alike needs to hear the Word of God. Everyone is required to respond in love to that call, from children whose understanding of Jesus is only beginning to elders whose basic theologies have been formed. The minister must understand that God's Word is a living Word, reaching with equal force everyone in the context of one's experiences. One avoids the frustration that winning youth to Christ is fundamentally dissimilar to that of winning adults.

Many pastors have been amazed to hear parishioners respond more favorably to gospel messages specifically geared toward the children than the messages geared toward the older church. This, too, points up the fallacy of trying to see two churches in the Christian church, one for youth and the other for adults. It also points us to the error of the statement "Youth represent the church of tomorrow!" The Christian church, whatever its strengths or weaknesses might be, is the church of right now. Therefore we look at some of the dilemmas in which ministers may become embroiled as they cope with childhood and youth myth expectations.

## Does the Minister Mix with the Children and Youth?

Nowhere in Scripture is the minister admonished to mix with children and youth. The focus of getting along and mixing with these age groups presupposes a certain barrier the gospel has to overcome. Nothing is further from the truth. Many leading biblical personalities made their mark with God in childhood and youthful experiences. The presence of baby Moses in a basket and our Lord in a crib takes precedence over any lullaby. Little David's triumph over Goliath and the youthful men and women around our Lord say something positive about the engaging demands of the gospel.

The minister as a servant of God has a certain positive image to uphold. That role does not demand nursery details or popularity contests with teenagers. The various callings and vocations of Christian ministry mean that some things should be done by others while weightier matters of faith are left to God's servant, the minister. The minister must not succumb to parental pressures for sociability and overlook legitimate pastoral authority. Once pastoral authority is lost among the people one serves, it is difficult indeed to regain. The minister cannot permit his or her calling to be judged by a pat on the back, give and take, and a wink of the eye. Fickle and foolish things crop up in matters of getting along. The personality responds positively or negatively on things of the flesh and not matters of conscience.

The Christian ministry has provided a beautiful approach to young people. Jesus used many illustrations based upon youth as concrete characteristics of true discipleship. "Verily, I say unto you, except ye be converted, and become as little children, ye shall not enter into the kingdom of heaven" (Matthew 18:2). It is hard for us to capture the full strength of Jesus' discourse. Children had no rights and were the property of their parents. The child was not a person in the full sense and was not expected to be self-assertive. *The Jerome Biblical Commentary* on this issue tells us that Jesus went on to identify with children and those who, in simple trust, gave their complete lives to God.

The church still wants to silence children and keep them from responding in self-assertive ways. Jesus stands over against this attitude, declaring that persons are persons, regardless of age or conditions. This is why Jesus stated, "Suffer little children, and forbid them not, to come unto me; for of such is the kingdom of heaven" (Matthew 19:14). It is in the ministering of little children that our Lord is received, even as he moves and lives in the lives of the adults.

It was a little boy who provided lunch for the hungry masses one day. Many ministers have thundered eloquently over how our Lord multiplied five barley loaves and two small fishes and fed five thousand men, besides women and children. (See John 6:1-14.) Seldom is much emphasis placed on the little boy. How did he feel about having to give up his lunch? Was he aware that his generosity had provided a blessing for everyone? Could he have known the Messiah made use of his gifts? Was he conscious that others had some food but hid it due to hardness of heart? A probing of these and other questions gives us a much larger picture of this young man who refused to be small and who participated in one of the great agape meals of the ages. No statues or commemorative days have been lifted in honor of this youth, but none can doubt his significant role in the Gospel narrative. The writer and beloved apostle John used that event to enlarge the spiritual lesson that Jesus Christ alone is the Bread of Life that satisfies the total need of everyone.

Many preachers, doctors, missionaries, evangelists, teachers, and servants of the people have heard God's voice in youth, asking the same question, "Is there any bread?" These persons gave their gifts, talents, and abilities to Christ and rose up to be great powers for God. Their lesson to us is clear, that every gift offered to God through Jesus Christ is blessed and returned bountifully!

## Youth and Christian Nurture

In Scripture the responsibility for training and nurturing youth rested upon parents. Fathers and mothers were expected to train their children in the tradition of the elders, the way of God, and the paths of truth. The community judged the parents if the children faltered in matters of faith. The proverb "The fathers have eaten a sour grape, and the children's teeth are set on edge" (Jeremiah 31:29) was aimed at parental responsibility. The family, the basic unit of Hebrew society, was expected to be a foundation worthy of interlocking with the wider society with justice and equity for all.

Jesus, a Jew, belonged to a family and was subject to its traditional controls. He gave his parents respect and obedience. His keen sense of divine mission at the age of twelve did not keep him from being "subject unto [his parents]" (Luke 2:51), after tarrying behind them in Jerusalem. The Hebrew home was a total human experience of worship, fellowship, work, arts, learning, and religion.

The Christian church is a legitimate extension of the biblical home, and the minister has the role of "spiritual leader." At home the child is expected to find oneself so as to participate with strength in society. The church provides the same substance, reaching deeper levels of the human soul. Moral principles are expounded, and the best in sacred tradition is lifted up. What has been learned at home is reinforced in the sacred family of the church.

It is a myth to assume that programs that express the desires of youth will hold them in the church and cause them to grow in Christ. No great traditions, culture, or mental discipline are needed to have a big dance, promote a rocking-chair party (as a fund-raising event), plan a pleasure trip, as wholesome as these activities might be. It is normal for youth to want to be involved in sports, parties, and social festivities. Yet we do not find these models in Scripture! Joshua and Caleb, David and Jonathan, Ruth and Esther, Paul and Timothy— all appear in Scripture from the days of their youth, rising up and leading forth in the name of the Lord!

The great church is one that offers first and foremost a solid ministry of Christ to everyone. Every life should be challenged to live its best! No legitimate desires of youth can be overlooked, but the church must do what it can do best! Molding lives and shaping character require a struggle to duty not demanded by worldly and pleasurable things. Organists do not play great church music overnight! Great preachers do not open their mouths and magical words jump forth! Youth must readily see a serious difference between the church and other agencies of society. Only then can the church rightly command the faith that ought to attend true discipleship.

The church that commands this faith must step beyond traditional bounds to nurture the growing lives of boys and girls. This was our experience at New Shiloh Baptist Church. In a congregation of three thousand worshipers, we knew that Christian education was woefully lacking. The usual weekly 9:00 A.M. to 10:45 A.M. Sunday school was reaching less than two hundred persons, adults included. What were the causes for our dilemma? We had dedicated teachers and a well-trained staff. We were a downtown church established in the hearts of many people. We used good literature, and money was not our major problem. Still we reached very few lives. We studied our problem collectively and concluded many things. Parents no longer had interest in their children learning the Bible as a basic requisite for living. Saturday nights in American homes no longer provided moments of bathing, cleaning and shining shoes in anticipation of worship on the Lord's Day. Television, shopping centers, disco-dance experiences, fast-food chains, and our mobile way of life had greatly reduced the importance of Sunday school for many families. Discovering all this led the New Shiloh Baptist Church to embark on an innovative Saturday church school program.

## Saturday Church School in Christian Nurture

New Shiloh's Saturday Church School program was not haphazardly planned nor suddenly put together. It was the development of a year-long search to find a better way to do the work of Christ. For some years I had held a "Saturday Neighborhood Youth Hour Program" where I had gathered with a fellow student minister and Christian worker to try through applied Bible teaching to reach young persons from around the church community. I must confess that during the year of our search for an innovative program, I longed to see our full staff think about Saturday as a day to give an in-depth work for youth in a Christian context. Toward the end of the year 1971, I made the suggestion that our church consider moving our entire church school work to Saturday, and challenged all workers, professional and skilled personnel, to join us and share their knowledge with others. The acceptance of that idea was overwhelming and produced a spirit of celebration.

We decided we would meet from 10:00 A.M. until 1:00 P.M. each Saturday. We agreed that we would strongly emphasize Bible knowledge; we were convinced that this was what our being was all about. Another period was given to elective courses, including electives in music, writing, arithmetic, cooking, typing, and whatever professional skills were available through dedicated personnel. One group called Youth Express, comprising a group of fifty or more teenagers, really caught and demanded attention. This class, led by a highly skilled worker with youth, has been able to ventilate and explore topics, no subject off limits, in an atmosphere of religious concern that has proved rewarding and constructive. It is almost impossible to get this group to end its vibrant discussions on time for worship, as the engaging topics led are plowed into by minds eager to know, to be heard, and to belong. In addition, there is a full community-wide Bible class taught by the minister. This program has permitted persons to come freely from all walks of life and study in a systematic in-depth way various topics and books of the Bible. The rewards for the minister have far exceeded the knowledge he has shared with others, since this exchange has kept alive seminary lessons and has given him sermon ideas to keep the Word of God fresh.

When the program began several years ago, some nine hundred pupils registered. Across the years the attendance has averaged between four and five hundred weekly. The program has had many positive and redeeming results, expected and unexpected. It has deepened the sense of missions and service for the entire congregation. It has provided a challenge for study and growth for youth that is difficult to refuse. Our findings show that many who would not ordinarily attend church on Sundays feel free to come on Saturdays. In time these persons become total members of church. Saturday has provided an unhurried time to give serious study to the many great issues of the Bible and to worship collectively in a relaxed and refreshing atmosphere. Many programs, following the emphasis of the Christian year, Christmas, Easter, and other special days, are celebrated with well-planned activities for this creative time. Above other things, the program has served as a source of great evangelism, reaching all age levels. Little did we know that this community-wide outreach would provide a ministry that would win so many to Christ! Youth have come, have become excited with the program, and have given their lives to Christ. Days later their parents have appeared before the altar, giving their hearts to Christ. All this has again proved the fact that young persons have a solid ministry to play in God's service when their lives are reached with power.

In matters of sports, star hitters are not heroes for being "bench warmers"; they consistently hit the ball. Great boxers are champions who deliver the knockout punch. Likewise, great ministers are those who have broken through myths that seek to order their lives and have become creative funnels for the ever-flowing grace of God. Youth can be met by ministries of churches that engage their beings beyond the experiences they receive on the outside. This calls for a presentation of Christ who says to every boy and girl, young man and young woman, "Play, enjoy life, but learn, grow, pray, and serve. You cannot do wrong and get by." There are some basic enduring needs of the human personality that can be met only through direct challenges of whether one will serve God or serve the world, be a follower of

Jesus' teachings about love or selfishly live and come to naught.

## Youth Need Adult Models

The models of adult Christians are an enormous influence for boys and girls. Adults who are genuinely human, biblically trained, socially sensitive, and willing to listen comprise that group the minister will surely need in order to reach today's youthful generation. The day of voluntarism in the church needs to be strengthened with the purposeful calling and dedication of persons who work and train themselves for their tasks.

There is a new breed of members in today's church who have never used their acquired knowledge in the service of the Lord. There are doctors and lawyers who have been programmed by professional procedures, who have not identified their skills with church work. Social workers, cosmetologists, culinary artists, and others comprise in most churches a cadre of people who could be challenged to share their testimonies and some of their skills with the people. These persons are in a position to say more than the mere words "God is good." Through their presence, they say to young persons, "lives can be polished into meaningful personalities that serve where others would be helpless!" Many times trained members have not become involved in community outreach projects in the church because they have not been asked. How many congregations have taken a few boys and girls to the doctor's office simply to see the doctor at work, or perhaps to the courthouse to see what happens to those who violate the law? These acts of relating youth to adult models are pressingly needed in today's urban centers. Dr. Roland Patterson, one of the regional superintendents of the New York City School System, said to me these words: "In my district, the great need is models. Boys and girls, eleven, twelve on up, are into drugs and dope. Many have died due to overdose. Who do they get their drugs from? The pushers, who could care less!" That same story can be repeated in almost any large American city and in smaller ones also. Boys and girls must know that an army of caring men and women are there, anxious to identify with them and show them another way. Time is late, and Christians must soon rise up and make use of all the church's power.

Generals and officers in the military are those persons who have mastered basic military skills and used their knowledge to instruct others to defend their country. They were disciplined! The church is a spiritual army. Generals, lieutenants, and officers are those who have dedicated their lives to Christ and find joy in leading others to him while waging war in the battle against sin. They provide the church strength through their mighty witness. Through living they say to young persons, "God is real; his word can be trusted; and he will provide for his own!" When these models are absent in any community, young persons will turn to other persons to find meaning, however tragic for their lives. Too often those persons are drug pushers, pimps, prostitutes, number writers, and persons not associated with the church.

When Martin Luther King, Jr., chose to resist wicked forces in the Montgomery protest of 1954, little did he know a great army of young persons would rise up and emulate his message and style. His strong, moral, forthright leadership left seeds that have already grown into directive service for much current leadership. A *New York Times* article entitled "Decade of Black Struggle: Gains and Unmet Goals," written after Martin Luther King died, stated: "More than half of all Southern blacks eligible to vote have now registered, a huge jump from the days of poll taxes and literary tests. . . . In 1968 there were only 250 black elected officials in the South. Today, there are 2,200, almost a tenfold increase."[1] In my own hometown of Selma, Alabama, "the heart of the Black belt," the same paper, dated April 3, reports this interesting account. A Mr. Tom Gilmore, now sheriff of Greene County, Alabama, told how the two forces, white oppression and the civil rights movement, shaped many Blacks in his generation. Mr. Gilmore in 1965 had decided to move north in search of work. En route, he was whisked by an Alabama state trooper who mistook him for one of the scores of demonstrators flocking to nearby Selma. "He put me up against a gas pump, and frisked me and unbuckled his gun. He said, '. . . I'm going to blow your brains out.' That's really when I decided to stay in Alabama. He made up my mind for me." Later this same young man became a field director for Dr. King's Southern Christian Leadership Conference, a job that put him in conflict with the white sheriff. By 1970 Mr. Gilmore had won his rival's job, and now he has deep aspirations of being the first Black congressman from the Black Belt, the heart of the Old South plantation country.[2] Mr. Gilmore's story is typical of persons from all walks of life, Black and white, whose lives were radically redirected by the movement and legacy of Dr. King.

Another leader of note, greatly inspired and influenced by Dr. King, is representative of the Seventh District of Maryland, and chairman of the Congressional Black Caucus. He stated to me these words: "Harold, we need great inspirational leaders. We need men after the mold of Mike King who live and teach the way of Christ. I hope you continue this thrust and never take down." Some days later, Congressman Mitchell worshiped in New Shiloh Baptist Church and thereafter wrote this letter, which I quote in part:

> My morale was very low when I got to church. All of the preceding week the House of Representatives had succeeded in passing crippling amendments to the Labor H.E.W. Appropriation Bill. . . . Amendments that would stifle Affirmative Action Programs, curtail civil rights enforcement. . . . Amendments designed to turn back the clock on the Blacks and the poor in America. I had fought hard against those vicious amendments but they passed. I was indeed dispirited when I came to church. Thanks to the magnificent singing, your truly inspirational sermon and the feeling of real fellowship in New Shiloh, I felt buoyed up, ready to return to the battles in Washington, ready to continue the fight.

Christ meant for his ministers to be empowering agents. Many meetings, caucuses, and places of gatherings will never be entered in person by ministers, but their Christ-filled influence can reach from the top of governments to the smoke-filled rooms where major corporate decisions are made. It is the vision of Christ that serves the fundamental force for good in the lives of all. "Deep calleth unto deep" is the psalmist's way of telling us God's witness causes persons to grow! This is why a forthright living of the Lord Jesus Christ makes an eternal difference in the growing lives of youth surrounded by adults exuding love.

## Youth Need a Rugged Christ

The Christian church has been less than candid in its presentation to youth of a Christ, stripped of human problems, never touched by the battering conflicts of life, moving in a kind of Being beyond everyday finite existence. Too often the true Christ, whom the church has declared to be fully God and fully Man, who liberated the captives and delivered the oppressed, has been misplaced by a sweet, spineless Jesus who offers nothing but quick happiness and blessings, one after another. A study of why many teenagers drop out of church reveals a lack of interest in subject matter. Why is this? Surely the study of Jesus Christ is a lifetime, demanding pursuit. Equally true is the fact that the Bible, a library of books, demands careful and rigorous mental toil. The problem is in the presentation of the subject matter. "Youth need a rugged Christ!" They need teachings, based upon Scripture, that engage them at least on the same academic level they are challenged in schools. This is not usually the case. Teachers can no longer come to church school class and assume a holier-than-thou attitude as being relevant to today's generation. This generation wants to know what you mean when you say, week after week, "Just be good children, and the Lord will bless you." Endless Christian cliches have lost so much of their power to a generation steeped in secular culture. Youth have seen the age of technology at work, delivering instant food, instant communication, and travel that appears almost instant. Yesterday's statements of faith must be rethought for this generation. A spineless Christ soon gets trampled upon in the parade of modern gods and self-proclaimed deities. Our guide has to be the same One who walked by the Sea of Galilee and said to some fishermen, "Follow me!"

When Jesus uttered the call to those fishermen, "Follow me," he expected unequivocal faith in his message and mission. He gave a rugged command and he expected a rugged response! Jesus knew there could be no positive Christian community without radical obedience to the demands of faith. It was an obedience that has its focus in God. No material goods were held out to lure these followers. No power to sway earthly masses for gain was expounded. Ideas of a pilgrimage of ease were never given by Jesus to lure anyone. His idea of discipleship demanded love that always authenticated itself through the love of God in the care of one's neighbor.

It would seem through the eyes of Hollywood that this call to people would not work today. Wall Street business persons, who devise all kinds of methods to sell their products, would call a strategy that tells people to deny themselves worldly comforts for higher and richer satisfaction "pure nonsense!" American churches caught in this awesome dilemma may have acquiesced beyond biblical grounds in presenting a Christ of culture and not a Christ beyond and above culture. Christ's statement "Follow me" was beyond culture when first proclaimed. Peter and all the apostles were not forged into some earthly empire, making them rulers of others, nor were they organized to fight and control others by might or power. They were called simply to be faithful to the demands of the kingdom of God. Out of the rugged commitment of a few early disciples, a universal church was established. That same church today needs a message rugged and without faltering worldly compromises!

Christianity's retreat from a rugged Christ demanding total allegiance may be one of the reasons so many young persons have taken to the streets, airports, and marketplaces, preaching saviors foreign to New Testament faith. Biblical scholars cannot applaud their many gods, but they cannot help but take notice of the military-like discipline through which these young persons present their gods. That same discipline ought to be turned toward the witness of Christ in a positive community way. Therefore a theology is sorely needed that will present Jesus Christ in his proper role, as Son of God, Lord of life, Savior of all, and final Judge of every soul. A proper balance between Jesus as Lord of life and champion of living would provide a healthier appreciation for God's world now and God's kingdom to come. God created this world, has a plan for it, sustains and executes that plan, and will one day fulfill it. God created music and gave persons the sense of sound, the gift of rhythm, the creative powers of sex, and ordered that all things were good in their proper places, sequences, and times! Youth will learn God's idea of a beautiful earth, with its minerals, vegetations, myriad firmaments above, and the care of fowl, cattle, and beast on plains and a thousand mountaintops! A rugged Christ will not demand learning the world, but living in divine harmony one with another in the world. Then marketplaces will be kissed with love for brother, sister, and everyone! Everyone will be part of the family of humankind!

The myth that Christ robs youth of pleasure and fun can be broken! It can be replaced by the truth that Christ alone brings life, love, liberty, and peace. He enlarges the capacity for living and ushers everyone into a fellowship of the redeemed. This attitude I speak about here was stated by a youth in a Saturday night crusade in New Shiloh Baptist Church. "I personally appreciate being in a church where our minister has kept to the Bible and made Christ real in my life. He may not know it; I am young, I know, and many think we look for something else, but I have noticed that our minister preaches Christ week after week after week," said Maxine Davis, a member of the church. I believe her testimony amplified a basic need for youth to hear the whole truth of the gospel. Youth need to be challenged to be Christians, by knowing and following the call of the Master.

The resurrection of massive youth witness is the most potent untapped arena the Christian church has in the battle for the hearts of the masses. History has shown youth's uncanny ability to wage war, create and lead movements, and to be heroes of faith. Ministers who zealously train disciples of youth for this age will invest in a crusade that will pay off. Satan and his henchmen of darkness and destruction will lose a mighty foothold when youth en masse can say, "Get behind me, Satan!" When they walk with God, they have the possibility of growing old with God. Christian roots can sink deep, pushing stalwart lives into God-fearing giants, ". . . while the evil days come not, nor the years draw nigh, when thou shalt say, I have no pleasure in them" (Ecclesiastes 12:1).

An effort has been made to suggest a new approach toward challenging Christian youth in today's world. From childhood through teenage years, youth need to know the rugged truth about Jesus and what he demands of their lives. Much of their knowing and responding is hinged upon the adult models they see and the teachings they receive. Wise ministers of the faith, knowing this fact, will lift up a Christ who is in culture, but always beyond culture. Youth will see their lives controlled by him and live out their days with a divine sense of love to God for the world and all there is, knowing that God's final kingdom is still to come. Having said this, let us then take a closer look at the world, spotlighting the minister and one's role in the community.

# The Civic Leader Myth

# 7

Traditional Christian ministry has oscillated between two extreme poles in its approach to the care of souls. The traditional evangelical approach believed the chief end of the gospel was converting the souls of persons from certain eternal death. This school of thought said humankind is alien from God, is a sinner, and can be saved only through acceptance of Jesus Christ as Savior and Lord of life. Once a person was saved, new life with God followed. The transcendent God saved humankind according to the unfolding plan of his providence worked out in life. The minister was God's chief spokesperson in this plan, calling those who would be saved to rise and follow the Master.

Another approach to Christian ministry has been the social approach to the gospel and the care of souls. Why change a person's soul only to see the person destroyed by an unjust social system? Biblically, social gospel ministers have modeled their work after the eighth-century prophets, whose ministry went beyond pulpits and altars, and who declared the Word of God even in the marketplaces. They believed God was concerned with the political systems that affected the lives of the people. Were the leaders honest, efficient, responsive to the needs of the poor? This social gospel approach has seen Jesus as a revolutionary leader, not merely preaching great truths, but living out fully those truths in life. Jesus is seen creating a new order for everyone, no longer based upon rank, racial heritage, male or female categories, but instead based upon one's relationship to God.

In today's world, social gospel advocates have gained a great deal from the theological school known as personalism. This school of thought blossomed in the ministry of Dr. Martin Luther King, Jr., who credited it as being his basic philosophical position. In a word, it believes that the clue to the meaning of ultimate reality is found in personality. Therefore God must be supremely interested in each person, each individual, since a clue to his own Being is locked in each self. Christ's death on the cross is the supreme example of love and selflessness that ought to be emulated by every person who dies to hate, malice, envy, and selfishness as one enters the kingdom of God.

Somewhere between these two positions, or at the extremes, each minister will seek to find one's position. There are some people who apparently want to be saved simply to await the rapture. Some want to be saved because it is now socially acceptable and does not demand much in return. Still others are striving for power and see the church as a step in their ambitious plans. Caught in the midst of all these groups, the wise minister will always operate from the church's base. Early in one's service, it is necessary to decide whether to minister or to be used as a minister.

## Ministering or Being Used as a Minister

When Jesus said, "Render unto Caesar the things that are Caesar's and unto God the things that are God's," he openly recognized that the state, as the church, demanded certain loyalties. The state demands a certain loyalty from its citizens to run the machinery of state, maintain civility, and serve the commonwealth. Knowing this, W. A. Jones, Jr., in a message at the Hubert Institute, Morehouse School of Religion, Atlanta, Georgia, 1977, stated, "Jesus never intended for us to wind up rendering almost all of our allegiance, all of our time and goods to Caesar!" All too often this is what happens. The dialectical tension between Christ and culture has a way of tilting the unsuspecting minister toward culture in a way that is nonproductive. Leading God's people out of the wilderness of selfishness, racism, poverty and war demands temporal involvements but a faith beyond temporal demands.

When the minister preaches the vision of the kingdom, the hopes of people are lifted. Equality based upon love is always revolutionary when heard by persons deprived of life's finer things. This is essentially what Jesus' accusers had in mind when they proclaimed, "He stirreth up the people!"

The minister does stir up people's latent visions and awaken in them the possibilities of better conditions, better living, and better communities. When these visions are stirred up, many look to the minister to be the leader of community uplift in such way that one's words are translated into institutions. Jesus' disciples wanted him to build a kingdom that would be akin to David's reign and would overthrow the yoke of Rome. People still want the minister to build kingdoms that will overthrow all the yokes that seem to choke their lives. Jesus was absolutely true to his Father while never ignoring humankind's temporal concern. The significant difference was that Jesus determined the course of his ministry among persons. That course was determined by a commitment to meet human needs and not build human empires.

Building God's kingdom on earth meant feeding the hungry, clothing the naked, visiting the prisons, and releasing the captives, in the theology of Jesus Christ. It meant acting out of a love not based on human motive, but on the basic fact that God himself is love. The people of God must love because everyone is a part of the potential family of God.

I believe Jesus came into Galilee in the beginning of his ministry preaching that the "kingdom of God is at hand," because it is necessary for the minister to know the exact building one is working on. In the eyes of the people, all kinds of prospects can assume kingdom proportions. Fraternities, lodges, sororities, and civic groups will often seek the minister and use the clergy to sanctify various undertakings. In such a group the minister is usually a good person, regular in attendance, and friend of all. Perhaps the minister might ask oneself, "How many of my civic friends are active in church? How many of them are motivated to actions by the Lord Jesus Christ? Do I feel free to lay upon them gospel demands?"

In setting up the church, Jesus immediately gave the apostles the key to the kingdom. Keys are used to unlock and secure doors. The minister's basic calling follows that given authority. With the Word of God, hard hearts are penetrated and bound spirits broken as doors of faith are opened! The same keys permit the minister to lock up and bind forever powers of evil working to assure Satan's reign. The minister can neither bind Satan nor release captive lives if one is a parrot for vested community voices. The servant must be free and constantly pray to God, "Lord, thy kingdom come!"

The minister escapes the civic leader myth by remaining free to witness wherever God directs. The coming of God's kingdom is not accomplished on a straight thoroughfare free of struggle and pain. The civil rights movement taught that the struggle for ethical demands has to be waged on many fronts, from Human Relations Councils and NAACP to attacks against evil and unjust wars. In this regard the holistic love ethic of Jesus Christ gives the minister a potent weapon to serve all persons under all conditions. Persons serve their neighbors in the absolute belief that the God of Jesus Christ is an infinitely Personal Being who is on the side of right and who will finally make the cause of good triumph. It is not the minister who brings the various dreams of persons to pass, for some of them may be out of harmony with God's program. The minister serves God faithfully, building ethical community among persons; and in the course of divine initiatives God's kingdom will come to pass.

Ministers ought to see themselves as agents of spiritual power enlisting and sending forth others in the ceaseless battle for truth. The struggle for good reaches all avenues of human existence, and someone is needed to touch humanity with the message of Christ. One type of person that ministers should work with is the politician. The minister must not permit oneself the cheap satisfaction of castigating other community leaders, particularly politicians. In our times a great deal of energy and words have been spent, pointing toward corruption in politics, as though all elected officials were crooks. The hour has come to take another look at this legitimate servant of God.

## The Tragedy of Denigrating the Politician

A major rationale giving rise to the idea that the clergy should involve itself in the political arena is the belief that politics is corrupt, mercenary, unregenerate, and debased. Granted, many political scandals have marred the political life, Watergate being the most notorious in recent times. What is overlooked is the politician's job to serve people. Like the clergy, the politician works to provide life support systems to enhance the quality of life. All fields of endeavor have at one time or another been marred by the acts and deeds of unscrupulous characters. Politician and minister, working to meet certain goals, can do so in mutual harmony and not deadening estrangement.

Dr. Scales, president of Wake Forest University, stated to a group of ministers in a seminar in Charlottesville, Virginia, 1976: "To try to come to Christian solutions on the public issues, without dividing fellowship, is the chief problem of our day." He stated that he now teaches a four-week course called Watergate. No less than 122 hard-covered books were out on the general subject of Watergate when he spoke, not to mention endless documentation and periodicals. One thing he required of his students was: "Put yourself on the other side of the fence. A Black student in my class chose to do a paper on Mr. Nixon. To her surprise, she had one major problem. She could find very little to undergird her thesis on 'The Positive Achievements of Mr. Nixon.'" Dr. Scales wanted to call us to see the other side of a life highly stereotyped in America as bad and evil.

The American dream as we know it represents the faith of pilgrims before us who placed their trust in elected officials and helped them work for the common good. Democracy has been the flowering expression of a people's finer selves, shared through their representatives to guard, protect, and insure the rights of all. This form of government, perhaps the noblest in all the world, could not have achieved the many triumphs it has, had the people been cynical and suspicious of those in public trust.

As a Black person born in the South and raised under the cursed system of segregation, I learned from my people the deep hopes, aspirations, and yearnings these people had as they looked to Washington to override and rectify unjust laws strangling their lives. It was this fundamental belief in democracy and the power of its laws administered through decent officials in high places that gave Black people a faith to work, pray, and seek for better days. They believed one day all persons would be able to run for elective office. One day society would be judged by the standard of mutual trust, persons working harmoniously together, and not by class standards or racial ghettos. Even now that dream is coming true. The eradication of unjust voting laws has made it possible for hundreds of minorities to be elected to public offices. Democracy presupposes that persons will have a sense of social decency and human goodwill to power the wheels of state. People must believe in the basic worth of humanity, the inalienable rights of the individual, the indomitable spirit of hope, and the infinite powers of life.

The apostle Paul addressed this subject. He told the Roman church that God alone was sovereign power and could share that power with whomever he pleased. Paul specifically stated that God shared his power with civil servants (Romans 13:4). Paul argued that ministers of church and ministers of state were both serving the necessary natures of humankind, both spiritual and temporal. Paul wanted to lift the Roman mind above the age-old schism of church versus state. Paul said, "Rulers are not a terror to good works, but to the evil" (Romans 13:3). Rulers who failed to see their missions as builders with God, discerning between good and evil, were just as guilty before God as clergy who denied the name of the Lord!

One of the chief reasons politics is denigrated in America is the apparent nationalistic desire to live one's life free of governmental interference. People want liberty without coercive arbitration. People want life-supporting services without the concern of programs often skyrocketing taxation. A degree of selfishness has fueled this feeling. In this age when citizens of every walk of life are inescapably locked together, there is that ancient enemy of the soul saying to each one, "Do it your way!" The Christian minister knows this is not so! The church, however strong, cannot long be strong without the state, and vice versa. All citizens have a divine right to render to Caesar but also to render to God. It is the faith commitment of life that tips the scales toward God and makes a difference that counts!

The minister, as a public spokesperson, can move from being an ambassador for God to being a critic for self. From the pulpit it is relatively easy to make politicians scapegoats for community sins. All kinds of civic problems can be publicly laid at the politician's door. People, already convinced that politics are dirty, will usually support these naive statements with unthoughtful "Amens." The very fabric of democratic life suffers. It suffers because a person is a collective being, and if his or her sister be ill, his or her life will suffer. Who gets the attention of the people, either the minister or the politician, is not a Christian issue. Jesus gave no examples of seeking a competitive role with other ministries of his day. That would have had the effect of legitimatizing the ways of the very persons Jesus wanted so much to convert. Everyone is part of the world order. Each must serve the common good according to the proportion of grace given by God.

What is needed is a working relationship between politician and preacher, saint and sinner, and the forging of a coalition of Christian conscience in times like ours. The jurist and lawyer still need a character witness, one who brings a word sanctioned by the Spirit of Christ. The mayor of the city still needs moral integrity and spiritual guidance if one's program is to reach and benefit people. The minister must speak to issues and problems which arise; the minister must go before the governor, the legislature, to declare one's support for programs like good housing, ecology, jobs, parks, even rehabilitative penal institutions. These are programs that need the support of all thinking people. As such, every person can be a minister of God. Otherwise, how can we meaningfully interpret Ezekiel's "wheel in the middle of a wheel"? (See Ezekiel 1.) All this the Christian minister can help to do, resisting the urge to set oneself over against another. The day has come for the minister to move beyond the myth that the clergy is the only servant of God the people can really trust.

## The Tragedy of Minimizing the Church

Along with the idea that politics are corrupt is the myth that the church is not relevant to meet today's problems. The local pastor must seek to find relevancy beyond church bounds to give vitality to one's work. Any ministry that is not seen in the streets, city hall, caucus rooms, and places where decisions are made is simply a nonchallenging echo of the status quo. This kind of thinking minimizes the church, the one divine source of power where fundamental changes can really be made. It is a natural course of action to move from denigrating the politician to minimizing the church and throwing one's hands into the air in helpless apathy.

It is difficult to see how President Jimmy Carter could have been elected president of the United States of America without the traditional respect for the Christian church in American life. This openly professing Christian publicly endorsed the works of Dr. Martin Luther King, Jr., and felt his indebtedness to the civil rights movement. In the height of Carter's campaign for the presidency, Dr. King, Sr., threw his arms around this man and declared his belief to the nation that this man was a leader worthy of public trust. The nation, faced with rising tides of social corruption, turned to the moral pronouncements of Mr. Carter and made him president against great odds. That historic event has noteworthy implications for the Christian church. The Reverend Jesse Jackson put it this way: "Harold, don't be fooled; I am admired by many, but I have no followers except those loyal to the church." Jesse Jackson knew that commitment to the church demands lifelong fidelity. People admire political leaders and movements for many reasons, good and bad. Politicians may be good looking, oratorical, wealthy, sociable, cunning, witty, romantic, and brave. Sometimes people get attached to various traits while ignoring the weaknesses of the leader. The Christian church by proclamation and practice should be different. People are called to build community around Christ. Dr. Martin Luther King, more than anyone else in modern times, spoke about the "Beloved Community." Dr. King believed the Beloved Community was a goal worthy of all Christians. It was this goal that made the church meaningful in his struggles.

> There must be a society that is not only free from the malformation of persons resulting from racial hatred but also free from the malformation of persons resulting from economic injustice and exploitation. Injustice anywhere is a threat to justice everywhere. Therefore economic and social liberation is basically a matter of justice and not of race. Justice cannot be seen apart from the indivisibility of human existence. Thus to King, the Beloved Community would reflect the intention of God, that all of his children should have the physical as well as the spiritual necessities of life.[1]

Only a limited theology views the work of the minister as confined to the perimeter of the local church. All life is sacred, and the church is called by God to reinforce that fundamental doctrine. There is no area of life where the church is off limits. The faulty theology of identifying the church only with the building, and ecclesiastical affairs in the building, is too narrow, too small. The church is forever prodded to remember heaven's declaration that "God loved the world and gave his Son!" It is easy for the church to say, "We love the Son and will refuse to share him with the world!" The true church of Jesus Christ gathers for worship, departs for service, gathers to hear the Word, departs to witness the Word, gathers to testify, departs to see new Red Seas open up and Jericho walls come tumbling down! The church is a marching band of disciples, headed for the city of God. No turf is off limits, and no souls exist that cannot be blessed with its message.

The Bible teaches that ministers denigrate the church when their faith is weak. Weak faith caused Peter to deny Jesus and follow afar off. Weak faith caused Demas to give up life's greatest romance for palatial and worldly comforts. People today cannot possibly know the true power of the church when the leader's faith is weak. A definite vision of God is necessary to see the Word changing the lives of countless masses, uprooting entrenched evils, and mending broken lives. There is a distinct need for practitioners of the faith to move from tabernacle to wilderness and tame the evils of life's uncharted ways. God still makes himself known in ways beyond the sacred walls and city gates. Red Seas, Jericho walls, lions' dens, fiery furnaces, and Isles of Patmos are all given to assure us that God is there when we need him most. Calvary took place beyond the temple, beyond the city's wall, to show us eternally that God is there!

The American church, blessed with so many means of communication, can still lead the way in getting this message out to all the peoples and ultimately to all the nations. From the beginning God's movement with his people has been community based, moving from one mountain to another. The mobile nature of the Ark and the tabernacle suited the needs of a nomadic people, passing this way but once. No wonder Jesus built no buildings and left no permanent shrines for his church! He built his church out of the living blocks of people's souls. The holding cement was "Jesus Christ, Son of God, Savior and Lord of life"!

A new bold theology of the church is distinctly possible with so much attention being given to current religious matters. Solving the problems of building human lives has proven too large for secular strength. A new theology of the church would provide full opportunity for men and women of all races. No longer would the church limit itself to four walls and a pulpit. This church would call persons to prayer, to face God wherever possible: a factory where people work, a park where some gather, a crowded marketplace where coins and bills are exchanged. When raindrops fall upon the earth, rivers eventually swell and the earth sprouts life. When the church fulfills its mission of reaching lives wherever found and of witnessing its faith in Jesus, the river of its communal stream will swell, and all God's people will share the blessings. "There is a river, the streams whereof shall make glad the city of God, the holy place of the tabernacles of the most high" (Psalm 46:4). Nothing in this world can take the place of or adequately substitute for the Christian church. It never loses itself flowing as streams in everyday life. In effect it carries out the Great Commission. Every stream of the church has "this treasure in earthen vessels, that the excellency of the power may be of God, and not of us" (2 Corinthians 4:7).

## The Pitfall of Proving Oneself

There is a big difference between making full proof of one's ministry and seeking to prove oneself. When Paul told Timothy, "Make full proof of thy ministry" (2 Timothy 4:5), he encouraged him to continue development in every aspect of his calling throughout life. He wanted Timothy to be single-minded in his pursuit of preaching Christ, living Christ, and building up the church, the visible body of Christ. Paul, out of wisdom, knew that many forces would try to sidetrack the noble efforts of this man of faith.

Dr. Elton Trueblood, the Quaker leader, gave me this advice at a time of personal need: "In order for you to develop your full creative abilities, and strengthen the powers of your mind, you will have to choose for a time many worthy programs you will not be able to involve yourself in. There are periods in one's life when one must be selective in order to one day perform an even greater service." I have lived to see the truth of those words, spoken to me in 1963. Now fifteen years later, with two accomplished academic degrees, and some definitive literature in print, I see how selective sacrifice of one's time can lead to deeper creative growth. The many calls for public service do not decrease with time, but tend to increase. It is easy to become a spokesperson for all kinds of community activities and to preach to a handful of interested souls on Sunday morning. When people do not see a clear image of the minister's base of power, the church and its proclamation, they will attempt to use one as the errand person of the community. Paul warned Timothy against this trap, knowing that Timothy's unique gift to minister could not be duplicated by others of his day.

The power structure of society has always known that if it could romance God's mouthpiece, the cause for righteousness would suffer. The power structures of countless American communities have used this method of placing leading voices for truth on their payroll, giving them official titles, making them commissioners of this study on that program. This deceptive promotion has usually silenced those soldiers of the cross who saw their elevation as an opportunity of a lifetime. The element of proving oneself is a strong emotional factor in this regard. Ministers feel good when they are granted entrance into governors' offices, big business rooms, city halls, and various civic planning boards. There is a legitimate place for the minister in these various centers. But let the minister go there as an Elijah free to speak to the Ahabs and Jezebels of his day and time, "Thus saith the Lord!" Let the minister go as an Amos, with no other powerful official backing than Yahweh—God, telling the Amaziahs and power structures of his day, "Set your house in order!" (See Amos 7.) The very people who find the minister succumbing to their traps to control one's voice will seek other spiritual powers in the crisis of their lives.

Mr. Alfred Burk, manager of WBAL, AM and FM, Baltimore, Maryland, was asked this question, "What is your disillusion with the church?" He answered, "I have deep trouble with a church turned social club. I still appreciate a ministry that represents God, proclaims his Word, and is not lifeless and cold. When I go to church, I want to be reached at soul level. I want to place my hands over flames of live coals and warm myself as a man coming out of the cold." Mr. Burk has shown great sensitivity to social causes through the powerful medium of communications, and he feels the church has greater power in the business community when it speaks free from vested interest.

This discussion raises the question, "Should the minister actively participate in political life?" The answer to this question follows the nature of one's calling. Previous discussion has sought to show that both civil servants and clergy are ministers responsible to God. Likewise, God can use the preacher in arenas other than the traditional church as a local meeting base. The real crux of the matter lies here. If one is going to give full service to political life, it might be wise to do that as a calling and not have the local flock suffer the absence of aggressive local leadership. Present days have shown us the possibility of many ministerial forms and roles. Ministerial voices in legislative halls, judicial rooms, wherever, can do profound good, as long as the clergy is convinced God has called it to the assigned task. Trying to answer the question of where the minister should serve, church or politics or some other way, has the effect of trying to circumvent the kingdom of God. No open mind can easily do that.

What is finally needed is that clergy will remember that "the kingdom of God comes first!" Additionally, the gathered church, wherever it may congregate, still provides for all persons the one visible witness of God's presence in life. Whatever models of new ministry may emerge, the gathered church will still have orthodox significance. Thus an appreciation for the power of the visible Body of Christ is an invaluable resource in the war for truth. "Where there is no vision, the people perish" (Proverbs 29:18). The creative church still demands a creative ministry, one demanding constant vigilance and nurture in order to have outreach and power.

We next take a look at "The Careless, Carefree Myth." This is a myth that leaves most ministers complaining, "How tired we are! Can't find time to rest, it seems." The problem of time and its effective use is a genuinely serious one. Organizing time and knowing where one is going demand disciplined maturity. Breaking the chains of this myth will unleash unexplored sources of creative energies and unlimited possibilities for the dedicated servants of God.

# The Careless, Carefree Myth

# 8

Jesus took great pains to show that the ministry was not a shelter for persons hiding from life's responsibilities. Every talent or ability given to clergy was expected to be spent in service, the secret of growth and spiritual development. Disciples had to leave everything—home, friends, social acquaintances—and follow the Master's call. No excuses were accepted from guests invited to attend the banquet supper. Everyone who heard the call to follow Christ and failed to do so forever lived under the weight of divine judgment.

The disciples around Jesus often felt that ministry was a place of ease, a life which would secure high seats in the kingdom. Peter had no clear idea of ministry when he said to Jesus, "Master, we have left all, and followed thee" (Luke 18:28). Peter had heard Jesus say to the rich ruler, "Sell all that thou hast, and distribute unto the poor, and thou shalt have treasure in heaven: and come, follow me" (Luke 18:22). Peter, the poor fisherman, saw the rich ruler as the packaged good life. He was educated, wealthy, religious, and young. Still, Jesus said he lacked something vitally needed for the good life. Peter was suddenly confronted with a radical idea of the good life. Jesus shifted the concept of wealth from the accumulation of wealth to the love ethic to share with others. All the disciples of Christ must have felt

like Peter. They could not make the transition from the possibility of
earthly wealth to spiritual power. Material possessions were more to
be desired than love services to the poor. They said to Jesus, "Who is
the greatest in the kingdom of heaven?" (Matthew 18:1). In private
conversations the disciples had already set up shadow cabinets that
would rule in pomp and power when Jesus finally moved to establish
his throne. Their secret plans leaked out when they said, "Grant unto
us that we may sit, one on thy right hand, and the other on thy left
hand, in thy glory" (Mark 10:37). Jesus answered both questions by
teaching the disciples that a cost had to be paid. They had to submit
themselves to God, humble as little children. They had to be baptized
with the spirit of service and sacrifice. Jesus promised divine
relationship. Jesus transformed their dreams of high seats into lowly
service, and in an upper room he washed their feet to teach love.

Notwithstanding, across the years the Christian ministry has
drawn many in search of ease and comfort. Some have gone so far as
to preach doctrines of material prosperity as proof positive of the
favor of God. Such a doctrine naturally justifies ministerial
profligacy and does violence to the redemptive call to suffering
servanthood.

In this chapter an effort will be made to examine how Jesus
overcame the "careless, carefree myth" and gave complete service to
his Father. Our study will confine itself to the temptation experiences
of Jesus, where certain radical commitments were made to God.

## Turn Stones into Bread

Satan zeroed in to the heart of Jesus' ministry during Jesus' long
fast in the wilderness. "If thou be the Son of God, command this stone
that it be made bread" (Luke 4:3). The subtle blow aimed at Jesus by
Satan was designed to induce self-doubt. Self-doubt would have in
time eroded the powerful relationship Jesus had with his Father. It
would have turned trusting faith into doubts and selfish flights. The
Christian minister must always be alert to one's relationship with
God. When that is estranged, the power for living and renewal is
gone! Jesus knew this and refused to succumb to this devious
temptation. The gospel ministry for our Lord was not a careless,
carefree experience. Yet this is one of the prevalent images Satan has
lifted before many who would preach.

Dr. E. V. Hill, minister of Zion Hill Baptist Church, and president of the California Missionary Baptist State Convention, told of this incident: "I was in Texas preaching. I met several seminarians. I invited three of them to come to Los Angeles to work summer jobs to aid in their theological growth. I arranged for them to begin on Sunday, all preaching in large churches. They were then scheduled to meet me Monday morning at 9:00 o'clock for further work assignments. On Monday morning I arrived at my office to await the ministers. No ministers came. They failed to come on Tuesday. Wednesday they did appear at the ministers' conference, dressed and looking good. They all asked me, 'Doc, where will we preach next Sunday?'" It is obvious those brothers had the wrong idea of what Christian ministry is all about. Dr. Hill had wanted them to do summer work with inner-city youth, to recruit and organize for Christian teachings and growth. They wanted just the opposite, ready-made platforms to come off as accomplished pulpiteers. They wanted to turn stones into bread without prayer, fasting, soiled hands, and manual labor.

Closely connected to this attitude is the one that suggests the Christian ministry provides instant success. If you have been a failure in other of life's pursuits, try the shortcut to the ministry, and all the folk will pay you homage. Turn stones into bread and eat without farm labor. Eat without shepherding the sheep or grazing the cattle. Such an action always violates the immutable law of God.

Laziness has a way of crippling creative ministry. It says to the minister, "You are tired; you must rest! You have all the people pulling on you, draining you of life. You must rest, rest, rest!" No wonder so many ministers almost unconsciously voice those familiar words, "I'm tired! If I just get beyond Sunday, or whatever event stares me in the face, I'll rest!"

Jesus had a secret out there in the wilderness. It was a deep trust in the word of God. It was an active belief that God's word was more fulfilling and life-giving than physical bread. Jesus would not permit physical bread to overshadow his need to obey God, even though his body agonized in hunger pains! He thought ideas beyond the carnal concerns of self.

How many ministers do just this? How many plan and execute creative hours of worship beyond the Sunday morning hour? How many ministers have taken the time to plan community outreach involving members of the church? How many ministers have sent Christian soldiers out to reach hungry masses in the name of Jesus Christ? If the minister has a laziness about one's mission, the church will surely catch it. If the minister leans on the pulpit, moves with no resolve, speaks with no enthusiasm, and just rambles through another worship, no one will be inspired, and laziness will be the lot of the whole church.

Laziness always tries to cover itself by turning stones into bread. It circumvents hard work, ignores creative abilities for sincere service, and uses itself to fool people. "Preparation for preaching is plowing the mind, turning it over so that fresh growth may appear. It is a long furrow. But whoever puts his hand to the plow and is not willing to go on to the end, with taut physical and mental muscles and a determined grip on the plow handles, is not worthy of the ministry." [1] All the trimmings of the church cannot hide the failings of one whose ministry is shoddy in the workroom.

I want to suggest several questions that might guide the minister in developing and maintaining a relevant Christian witness. The first question to be examined is, "Is the minister reaching lives for Christ?" Churches will worship the vision that is held up by the leader. Thus churches can turn inward and worship themselves. Some worship their ministers, their pastors. A church alive in the biblical tradition of faith has a spirit of Christian love, a love of prayer, a desire and readiness to serve human needs, and is committed to making Christ real in the world. The theme that runs through every page of this book guiding the minister beyond the low ground of deathly myths is Christ. When Christ is absent in one's ministerial pursuits, the building will eventually come down.

A second question the minister ought to ask oneself is, "Are lost souls being continuously reached and converted to the way of Christ?" This concern generated into the lives of worshipers who fill the pews will make a mighty difference! When the members start talking about missions, reaching people, building lives, the church has caught fire! People's conversations are fairly accurate barometers of what the life and purpose of the church is.

A third basic question is, "Who beyond the walls of the church is being helped through this corporate witness?" The flock of Jesus

Christ is vastly larger than the gathered few on Sunday mornings. Visions limited to the local church are too small, too narrow, too exclusive! Theoretically speaking, the whole world is the minister's parish. Jesus said, "Go ye therefore, and teach all nations, baptizing them in the name of the Father, and of the Son, and of the Holy Ghost: Teaching them to observe all things whatsoever I have commanded you: and, lo, I am with you alway, even unto the end of the world" (Matthew 28:19-20). The local church is the base, the foundation that gives strength to a wider work for Christ.

A fourth question the minister might ask is, "In what way does my ministry relate to other ministries of Jesus Christ?" Am I working in fellowship with my association, convention, denomination, of which I am a part? Where possible, am I helping ecumenical causes that build the walls of Zion and help to break down walls of partition? "We know that we have passed from death unto life, because we love the brethren," said John (1 John 3:14).

A fifth probing question is, "What is the burden of my prayer life?" Prayer growth can easily be neglected or at best relegated to the least essential demands of the mighty Christian faith. Jesus' life revealed that prayer was paramount and required more than rote recitations, but demanded a discipline to listen to and follow the will of God. An indictment of the present age may be its failure to listen adequately to God!

A sixth question is equally important: "What do I do with my leisure time?" Have I ceased to grow mentally and spiritually? Are theological developments and issues still important to my ministry and exhortations? If we postulate that God is love and is involved intimately in the human arena, then questioning minds must constantly search and seek to know where God is making his moves! Watching and praying are total demands for effective and spirit-filled ministry.

A seventh question would be, "Is my ministry effectively received at home?" Something is wrong if I can minister to others but am an outcast in my own home. One's family can reflect in depths the impact one's ministry is having on the larger world, through everyday actions and deeds.

All of these questions will help the minister keep before oneself the vision, the tools, the labors of love necessary to feed the sheep of God a well-prepared diet of God's Word. Stones will not be turned into bread, because the way of God is always greater than shortcuts offering quick meals with lasting spiritual indigestion.

## Jump Down from the Steeple

The minister of Christ charged by public acclaim is tempted to be a crowd pleaser. How can I grab public attention and steal the show? "If thou be the Son of God, cast thyself down from hence: For it is written, He shall give his angels charge over thee, to keep thee: And in their hands they shall bear thee up, lest at any time thou dash thy foot against a stone" (Luke 4:9b-11). Satan again used his "if" method and added to it the record of Old Testament Scripture to try to deceive our Lord. (See Luke 4:9-12 and Psalm 22.) Had Jesus jumped down from the steeple, the vision of Isaiah's Suffering Servant would have been shattered and human redemption would have vanished in passing popularity. Jesus refused to jump down!

The eternal laws of God are now broken because of people's shortcomings and earthly failings! Many ministers see the kingdoms older ministers have built and want an even greater kingdom right now! It is difficult for them to separate personal development from public acclaim. The public, anxious to receive a word from God, any kind of a word, will receive almost anyone under certain conditions. Thus it is possible to jump down from lofty positions. See the clergy with prayer cloths, providing illicit numbers for lotteries and passing out blessings for material gains. Music, all jazzed up, and given out without regard for theology or message, is another way of jumping down to lure the masses. Entertaining preaching with no prophetic content, no calling of people to discipleship, gets the applause of Satan for a season.

These temptations of our Lord with Satan are important in that they reveal the length to which Jesus went before he had to say "No" to evil! It was no quick decision but involved all the totality of his being. Stewards of Christian ministry overcome carefree myths by remembering that nothing redemptive in life comes free!

Jesus' response to Satan's temptation was aimed at the center of the attack: "Thou shalt not tempt the Lord thy God!" Jesus lifts life to a higher level. Let one's major task be so consuming that lesser temptations will not prevail!

That higher level for the minister could well be preaching. Preaching is the unique force of the Christian faith! It is the chief way of winning lost souls and building up dedicated lives! It is the most effective tool God has given to us to build up fellowship and miraculously to see the Word become flesh! When preaching is relegated to a lesser activity of the church, the people suffer.

Jesse Jackson was asked the question, "Do you still enjoy preaching?" He responded with these words:

> It is the supreme joy of my life. . . . I think when I was a little younger, I may have preached for reputation; but the older I get, I preach for edification. And when I see the crowds come in, I don't feel so much good as I feel obligated. They come from so many walks of life, and they expect so much. A lot of them don't come to church ordinarily; and so to have prepared myself as best as possible as a vessel through which the Word of Truth might come is a very obligative state of existence.[2]

The minister can learn from others who have had great public lives. Elvis Presley is a case in point. *Time* magazine, writing about his meteoric popularity, stated, "So the legend goes: nothing kills America's culture heroes as quickly and surely as success. Presley burnt himself out, as if on schedule." Speaking about himself, Presley said, "I am a house rocker, a boy steeped in mother-love, a true son of the church, a matinee idol who's only kidding, a man with too many rough edges for anyone ever to smooth away. Something in me yearns for a settling of affairs."[3] Presley's words reveal a dilemma of finding himself locked in a world too far from reality to get back! How does one get back when one has jumped from life's high pinnacles and broken one's limbs? Jump from one steeple and survive, and the law of instant success demands a second jump until tragedy claims its own!

While Elvis was not a minister and made no ministerial claims, he did evidence a love for his early church training. He said it was one of the forces in his life, among many other forces! His testimony ought to help the minister see the hazard of trying to keep many candles burning in one's life at once. The Judaic Christian God is a righteously jealous God and will not tolerate shared fidelities. The way of the cross may not compare to the popularity of the steeple, but the cross endures because it was sanctioned by God.

Jumping down from life's high places presupposes lofty positions.

The devil took Jesus to the high steeple of Jerusalem's temple. This strategic location was the high point of any potential publicity. It was like being in today's New York City, with someone about to jump from the Empire State Building. No Capernaum or Jericho or Nazareth would do for this event. Throngs of pilgrims were always present to see and report happenings. Jesus might have thought, *The people know that the temple is God's house and a successful jump would prove me God's Son. This is my moment, this is my opportunity!* Jesus refused to jump!

The life and love of Jesus Christ places every minister on a lofty platform. The perfect life, the perfect sacrifice, the perfect redemption of Jesus Christ is the foundational insurance people see in the one who ministers. This is why it is a scandal to take advantage of this high call for personal glory and secular acclaim. All glory belongs to God. Ministers are called to be partakers with Christ of his sufferings, sacrifices, and ways of love. The gifts of God take one infinitely higher than physical steeples, providing one can resist steeple temptation. God wants to entrust hungry masses to his servants, so they might be filled. God wants civil leaders, with legal power over people, to hear saving words. Someone must be high enough to be seen by many, yet low enough to resist demonic temptations to fall. Still, Satan is not finished.

And the devil said unto him, All this power will I give thee, and the glory of them: for that is delivered unto me; and to whomsoever I will I give it. If thou therefore wilt worship me, all shall be thine. And Jesus answered and said unto him, Get thee behind me, Satan: for it is written, Thou shalt worship the Lord thy God, and him only shalt thou serve (Luke 4:6-8).

## Get Thee Behind Me, Satan

Jesus always evidenced a decisive ability to act quickly in times of need. That ability was strengthened by Jesus' understanding of evil as an ever-present reality. Evil was not lost in intellectual gymnastics and endless debates. Satan was real, but so was God! Satan sought to control the earthly kingdom while God controlled both heaven and earth. A decision had to be made as to who would really be God. Ignoring satanic power was not the way of Christ. Satan could bind human lives and subdue human spirits. Fighting Satan on human powers alone was sure defeat. Fighting Satan with a resolve to choose

God and say no to Satan's kingdom was the only way of life. It was this determination that led Jesus to say, "Get thee behind me, Satan!"

"Worship me and servants will wait on you; chefs will cook delicacies to please you; musicians will play lullabies to thrill you while beautiful women with luscious bodies dance before your eyes. Worship me, Jesus, and I will make all nations subject to your rule and responsive to your voice," Satan entices. There is always grave danger in identifying the world with Satan's ownership. When wicked establishments can argue a difference between church and state, they can do their corrupt works without prophetic judgments. This is why historically many have argued that the church has no business lifting its voice beyond sacred walls. The argument suggests that God has titled the nations over to Satan. That is not so!

The vanity of the world is only a meaningless temptation. All of us are tempted to vanity, particularly if some success has attended our ministry or if we have, in fact, something more than modest gifts as a preacher. We are tempted:

1. To recline
2. To shine
3. To whine.[4]

Satan manipulates vanity in such way as to ensnare every budding ministry. The minister, being something of a little god in the midst of the people, must resolutely flee temptations to wield big chains of power, to shine in liturgical splendor, and to whine away the awesome problems of life.

Why be a little god anyway? Jesus chose the opposite way. Being God, he chose total humility, total servanthood, "and was made in the likeness of men: and being found in fashion as a man, he humbled himself, and became obedient unto death, even the death of the cross" (Philippians 2:7-8). Humankind is locked into the nature God has given. That nature includes infinite possibilities for service and self-transcendency, but to be God is beyond human powers! Only God can be God! One does not by choice decide to rule over the world. All power belongs to God, and persons' uses of that power come through the path of humility. "Ye know that the princes of the Gentiles exercise dominion over them, and they that are great exercise authority upon them. But it shall not be so among you: but whosoever will be great among you, let him be your minister" (Matthew 20:25-26).

One cannot tell Satan to get behind one's life unless one is reaching forth to help fallen humanity. Satan occupies sinners and fills dangerous voids. When one does not have the focus of one's work in view, the sense of going forward or backward is blurred. "Get thee behind me, Satan," permitted Jesus to leave the mountain of temptation and go to his hometown of Nazareth and deliver the following discourse:

> The Spirit of the Lord is upon me, because he hath anointed me to preach the gospel to the poor; he hath sent me to heal the brokenhearted, to preach deliverance to the captives, and recovering of sight to the blind, to set at liberty them that are bruised, to preach the acceptable year of the Lord (Luke 4:18-19).

From the mountain to Nazareth, Jesus focused upon his ministry. Following our Lord demands that kind of commitment to duty, building the work of the kingdom.

"And when the devil had ended all the temptation, he departed from him for a season" (Luke 4:13). The temptation to careless living and carefree responsibilities is not conquered in a single victory. The battle of evil is lifelong. While battles may be won, victory is assured only through the work of Jesus Christ. This means that ministers cannot rejoice too long over triumphant satanic battles. Every transfiguration experience has the challenge of a valley of human suffering. God works in a mighty way among people. Where the sick are found, healing will take place. Where people's lives are enslaved and justice abused, God still liberates. Many shun the valleys of suffering, but they do so to the death of their own blessings and experiences.

My faith in the relevancy of Jesus' life for humanity grows brighter and stronger day by day. Many of the gods of today's world, like Humpty Dumpty, have fallen. Devotees of these gods are unable to put them back together. A Baltimore mother in a political forum meeting asked the speaker these words: "What can you do for me? I have a son who at twenty-one years of age is totally alcoholic. He no longer respects his mother." It occurred to me that all the political leaders of the nation could not finally solve this mother's problem. All the people in business with their know-how, apart from Christ, do not have a solution for her. That mother approached the meeting as the father who brought his son to the apostles in need of healing. The apostles failed the man. (See Luke 9:39-42.) I could not help but wonder whether the institutions of humanity today are failing humanity. The only place on planet Earth where that mother's problem ought to find healing is the church. It can restore broken lives! It can restore mothers who may be partly responsible for the downfall of children. It can restore fathers who have lost their way.

The person of Jesus Christ is the only all-sufficient One. He has unleashed enough power to save every potential soul who will look and live! He has provided enough grace to forgive every lost soul, ever to be born and live! He has provided enough blessings to delight every heart and to cause every believer's cup to run over! He has given enough glory for every disciple to shout "Holy," and declare God's name above all! Jesus Christ only is the all-sufficient One! Any complaining minister belies one's own faith and reveals one's own weakness! Any minister broken by temptations reveals one's own insufficiency of trust in Christ, relying on one's own crippled legs! Abiding in Jesus is the secret of faith. His life, his death, his resurrection from the dead, his loving concern and constant intercession break through when he is the Branch and we are vines! This ever-present Christ turns servants of his into angels of light, rising high above one's greatest dreams, in mighty, ever-flowing spiritual power, proclaiming the year of jubilee and ringing loud the bells of salvation.

# Summary and Conclusion

# 9

      This book has been written for the purpose of sharing with the Christian ministry and the church at large sober reflections which I have found meaningful through ministerial experience. It has been given in the belief that we grow as we share our knowledge and insights one with another. Whatever anyone can do that will help to lift higher the matchless banner of Christ ought to be done without delay. The Christian ministry should seek the best in spiritual devotion, mental training, bodily discipline, and leadership qualities. Reaching the best demands a knowledge of one's calling and of some of the pitfalls to be avoided.

      After one announces one's call to preach, the job of ministering has only begun. Seminary training will sharpen the mind and provide much needed information. Notwithstanding, each minister, like Moses, will have to walk the uncharted paths of rugged wilderness experiences. Prophetic loneliness will often grip the soul as one moves through the maze of human encounters, trying to provide meaning for life. The nature of ministerial faith demands a certain unfolding of events and the coming to light of baffling problems and complex human conditions. Finding theological authority demands more than a profound announcement to preach. Images and styles of personal behavior will prove too thin to hide the need for substance and power with God. Every minister would be wise to go beyond crippling myths, discussed in this book, offering many promises while guaranteeing no godly power.

There will always be myths, espoused by others, and guaranteed to ensure ministerial success. Some ministers, like Demas who for a while walked with Paul, will leave the path of faith to bathe in worldly splendor. Many see themselves as profound and zealous leaders, simply because these myths always present half truths. They refuse to tell the whole story! They have a word for the minister at every turn of one's life. They tell the minister, "Forget the books, tell the people about Jesus; how will they ever know the difference?" "Don't listen to the people; you are the boss of this church! God has placed you in charge and given you the power!" The outward progression of these myths tells the minister that this life is public. You can do as you please since you belong to the people. Use men or women to support self-made kingdoms and short-lived empires. Use whatever power you can swing to draw more persons under your influence. You are the boss of the city, the kingpin, the one whose words must be consulted before programs can move off dead center. This type of minister is usually charming and dapper. One tries to be regular with the youth, often permitting them to do their own thing. In a word, this is a careless, carefree ministry publicly announcing a commitment to Christ, but privately mapping one's own strategy of faith.

It would seem that the foregone descriptions of Christian ministry are absurd. That is not the case. Public and private pressures in the ministry cut deep! Long traditions have a way of sanctifying evil practices. The myths discussed in this book have all had their day in history and remain sufficiently alive to influence many modern-day souls. This book has attempted to expose their power and call forth a new and bold cadre of Christian ministerial soldiers who would reassert the Christ of the ageless and battered cross of Calvary.

The Black minister especially needs to overcome these crippling myths as one ministers in an age of golden opportunity. So many Black lives are housed together in congested urban centers. So many hopes, dreams, fears, agonies, frustrations, and still spiritual yearnings are there in need of proper direction. God has historically made himself known, in unique ways, where people lived together en masse and in great need. Any effective Christian ministry must still start and end with God! A relevant Black ministry, supported by concerned White clergy, would work together to continue the fervor of the church's love for Christ. Definite ways would be found to win lost souls to Christ. Oftentimes basic evangelism is overlooked and considered invalid in our present-day rush to appear relevant on social issues. Salvation in the Body of Jesus Christ is still basic and absolutely necessary for the proper development of all other aspects of one's life. This team ministry of faith and power would find ways to represent the people and articulate their needs for jobs, good housing, and the freedom to participate by sharing the full menu of the banquet of life.

This creative team ministry would not be limited to the local church. Through minister's conferences, alliances, associations, and conventions, Christ would be exalted; a standard of holiness would be raised; and many in need would be benefited. Urban centers would rejoice and blossom as roses. Highways of life would be built instead of endless lanes of cement that transport so many up and over human need. Any genuine Christian fellowship must still clothe the naked, feed the hungry, release the captives, and set the prisoners of sin free.

Doing all of this will require a new understanding between pastor and politician. The politician and minister ought to stand side by side building strong walls of human service. Both are ministers of God and serve the commonwealth of humankind. One needs the other in the common cause for good.

Delegate Larry Young, representative to Maryland's House of Delegates, 1977, said, "If politics are to be cleared up, if government is to remain in the control of the people, then more men and women, particularly those who are Christians, must become politicians or support vigorously those who by their work demonstrate a Christian witness!"[1]

The minister can be an ambassador of God to empower others to go where one cannot go and do jobs off limits to one's calling. From the pulpit and through day-by-day contacts, the minister can counsel, challenge, inspire, and provide courage for political workers and all others who serve the present age. God's house is a place for finding strength, and the minister must be that fresh water conduit to funnel living waters to the dying of this age. Young ministers have an exceptional opportunity to marry intellect with prophecy, spirit with substance, style with service! The power of the living God administered through the living Word is still this world's greatest salvation.

As long as there are people, God will call someone to preach to them his Word! What one does after one receives the call is largely determined by commitment and sincerity of faith. Sitting next to Dr. D. E. King in a convention meeting recently, I asked him whether a certain minister I did not know too well could preach the Word. Dr. King responded, "When it does not get out that one can preach, you need not ask if one can." The Word effectively preached cannot be hid, neither can a life effectively sold out into the service of Jesus Christ. A city set on a hill cannot be hid, neither can a life ablaze with the glorifying works of Christ. We do not have eternity to live. Measured against eternity, our lives on planet Earth are rather brief. Still that brevity provides sufficient time for learning Jesus, living Jesus, lifting Jesus, loving Jesus, and ever longing for the triumphant return of Jesus! This is the hope that triumphs over the myths of the world! This is the faith that exalts a nation! This is the path that assures the victorious life.

# Notes

## Chapter 2

[1] Raymond E. Brown, *The Jerome Biblical Commentary* (Englewood Cliffs, N.J.: Prentice-Hall, Inc., 1968), p. 49.

[2] As quoted in David Thomas, *The Homilist* (New York: N. Tibbols and Sons, 1876), p. 267.

[3] W. W. Melton, *The Making of a Preacher* (Grand Rapids, Mich.: The Zondervan Corporation, 1953), p. 18.

[4] C. E. Colton, *The Minister's Mission* (Grand Rapids, Mich.: The Zondervan Corporation, 1953), p. 129.

## Chapter 3

[1] Lloyd John Ogilvie, *You've Got Charisma!* (New York: Abingdon Press, 1976), pp. 30-31.

[2] Elton Trueblood, *The New Man for our Time* (New York: Harper & Row, Publishers, Inc., 1970), p. 113.

[3] "Religion in the News," *The Chicago Tribune,* Saturday, July 9, 1977, Section 1, p. 13.

[4] Trueblood, *op. cit.,* p. 83.

## Chapter 4

[1] Thomas Kilgore, "Walking the Edge of the New," annual address, Progressive National Baptist Convention, August 11, 1977, p. 7.
[2] Taken from an interview by the author with N. W. Norwood, August 26, 1976.
[3] Edward C. Devereux, Jr., "Gambling Goes Legit," *Time* magazine, December 6, 1976, p. 56.
[4] *Ibid.*
[5] Quote taken from a Conference on Evangelism, New Shiloh Baptist Church, Baltimore, Maryland, April 4, 1978.
[6] Bill Adler, *The Wisdom of Martin Luther King in His Own Words* (New York: Lander Books, Inc., 1968), p. 109.
[7] Paul Cowan, "Jesse Jackson: The New Black Dream," *The Village Voice,* vol. 20, no. 9 (March 3, 1975), p. 7.
[8] Quoted from a lecture given by Dr. Carlyle Marney at Morris College, Sumter, South Carolina, May, 1977.

## Chapter 5

[1] The Fund of Renewal is a jointly sponsored program of American Baptist Churches and Progressive National Baptist Convention to support minority causes financially. This statement was taken from a sermon Dr. James Peters gave at New Shiloh Baptist Church, Baltimore, Maryland, January 30, 1977.
[2] Wolfhart Pannenberg, *Jesus—God and Man,* trans. Lewis L. Wilkins and Duane Priebe (Philadelphia: The Westminster Press, 1974), pp. 73, 77.
[3] Kenneth A. Briggs, "Jewish Scholars Reassessing Historical Jesus," *New York Times,* February 2, 1978, p. B 1.
[4] "Yeshua Is the Messiah," *Time* magazine, July 4, 1977, p. 76.

## Chapter 6

[1] "Decade of Black Struggle: Gains and Unmet Goals," *New York Times*, April 2, 1978.
[2] "Black Political Revolution in the South," *New York Times,* April 3, 1978, p. A 16.

## Chapter 7

[1] *Debate and Understanding,* Semester Two (Boston: Boston University, 1977), p. 147.

## Chapter 8

[1] Halford E. Luccock, *In the Minister's Workshop* (Nashville: Abingdon Press, 1954), p. 211.

[2] "You Can Pray If You Want To," an interview with Jesse Jackson, *Christianity Today,* August 12, 1977, p. 13.

[3] "An American Legend: Elvis Presley 1935–77," *Time* magazine, August 29, 1977, pp. 56-58.

[4] David Christie, *The Service of Christ,* quoted in Edgar Dewitt Jones, *The Royalty of the Pulpit* (New York: Harper & Row, Publishers, Inc., 1951), p. 286.

## Chapter 9

[1] Quoted from a letter from Larry Young to the author, August, 1977.